PHONICS IN PROPER PERSPECTIVE

EIGHTH EDITION

Arthur W. Heilman
Professor Emeritus
Pennsylvania State University

Merrill,
an imprint of Prentice Hall
Upper Saddle River, New Jersey   *Columbus, Ohio*

Library of Congress Cataloging-in-Publication Data

Heilman, Arthur W.
    Phonics in proper perspective / Arthur W. Heilman. —
    8th ed.
      p. cm.
    Includes bibliographical references (p.) and index.
    ISBN 0-13-614645-7
    1. Reading—Phonetic method.   I. Title.
LB1573.3.H44   1998
372.4145—dc21   96-39449
                                     CIP

Editor: Bradley J. Potthoff
Production Editor: Linda Hillis Bayma
Copy Editor: Genevieve d'Arcy
Design Coordinator: Karrie M. Converse
Text Designer: Angela Foote
Cover Designer: Proof Positive/Farrowlyne Assoc., Inc.
Production Manager: Patricia A. Tonneman
Director of Marketing: Kevin Flanagan
Advertising/Marketing Coordinator: Julie Shough

This book was set in Frutiger Light by Carlisle Communications, Ltd. and was printed and bound by Quebecor Printing/Book Press. The cover was printed by Phoenix Color Corp.

Earlier editions © 1989, 1985, 1981, 1976, 1968, 1964 by Macmillan Publishing Company.

Printed in the United States of America

10 9 8 7 6 5

ISBN: 0–13–614645–7

Prentice-Hall International (UK) Limited, *London*
Prentice-Hall of Australia Pty. Limited, *Sydney*
Prentice-Hall of Canada, Inc., *Toronto*
Prentice-Hall Hispanoamericana, S. A., *Mexico*
Prentice-Hall of India Private Limited, *New Delhi*
Prentice-Hall of Japan, Inc., *Tokyo*
Simon & Schuster Asia Pte. Ltd., *Singapore*
Editora Prentice-Hall do Brasil, Ltda., *Rio de Janeiro*

PREFACE

The purpose of this book is to provide both the experienced and the prospective teacher with materials that will lead to better understanding of the following:

- The purpose and limitations of phonics instruction as it relates to teaching reading
- Concrete practices to follow in teaching the various steps in phonics analysis
- The rationale that underlies particular instructional practices

The material in this book reflects several premises:

- Phonics is an important part of teaching beginning reading.
- Teachers should be knowledgeable about the purpose of phonics instruction and its limitations.
- For children to make normal progress in learning to read, they must learn to associate printed letter forms with the speech sounds they represent.
- Beginning reading instruction must not mislead children into thinking that reading is sounding out letters, or learning sight words, or using context clues.

Learning to read involves *all* these skills in the right combination. The optimum amount of phonics instruction for each child is the absolute minimum the child needs to become an independent reader. Excessive phonics instruction will usurp time that should be devoted to reading, can destroy children's interest in reading, and may lead critics to attack phonics instruction rather than bad phonics instruction.

For the eighth edition, I would like to thank the following reviewers, who provided valuable comments and suggestions: Anne Marshall Huston, Lynchburg College; Nancy B. Keller, State University of New York, Oneonta; William S. O'Bruba, Bloomsburg University; and Betty D. Roe, Tennessee Technological University.

CONTENTS

PHONICS: PURPOSE AND LIMITATIONS

The purpose of phonics instruction is to teach beginning readers that printed letters and letter combinations represent speech sounds heard in words. In applying phonic skills to an unknown word, the reader blends a series of sounds dictated by the order in which particular letters occur in the printed word. One needs this ability to arrive at the pronunciation of printed word symbols that are not instantly recognized. Obviously, if one recognizes a printed word, he should not puzzle over the speech sounds represented by the individual letters.

"Arriving at the pronunciation" of a word does not mean learning *how* to pronounce that word. In most reading situations, particularly in the primary grades, the readers know the pronunciation of practically all words they will meet in their reading. What they do not know is that the printed word symbol *represents* the pronunciation of a particular word they use and understand in oral language. Through phonic analysis they resolve this dilemma. Phonic analysis is an absolutely essential skill in beginning reading.

THE STUDY OF PHONICS

Phonics is not a *method* of teaching reading, nor is it the same as phonetics. Phonics is one of a number of ways a child may "solve" words not known as sight words. Phonics instruction is concerned with teaching letter-sound relationships *only as they relate to learning to read.* English spelling patterns being what they are, children will sometimes arrive at only a close approximation of the needed sounds. They may pronounce *broad* so it rhymes with *road,* or *fath* (in father) so that it rhymes with *path.* Fortunately, if they are reading for meaning, they will instantly correct these errors. After a few such self-corrections, they will never again make these particular mistakes.

Phonetics is much more precise. It is the scientific study of the sound systems of language. Phoneticians are scientists. They know much more about speech sounds and spelling patterns than is necessary for children to know while learning to read, or for teachers to teach when the goal is teaching reading.

Linguists rightfully urge reading teachers not to confuse phonics with phonetics. Phonetics is a science; the teaching of reading is not. While it is true that phonics is based on phonetics, linguists should not be distressed when they observe a phonics instruction program that does not include certain known phonetic data. First and second graders do not need to be exposed to all the phonetic data that have been assembled. Learning to read is a complicated process, and it need not be complicated further simply because a vast body of phonetic data exists. In teaching reading, one must hold to the scientific principle that instruction must follow the most economical path to its chosen goal. A guideline for instruction is that *the optimum amount of phonics instruction a child should be exposed to is the minimum the child needs to become an independent reader.* This is certainly not the way to become a linguist, but it is good pedagogy for beginning reading instruction.

Terminology

In recent years, noticeable confusion has accompanied discussions of reading because the meaning of some of the terms used has been vague or misleading. To eliminate further confusion, we will briefly define a few basic terms.

Alphabetic principle. Graphic symbols have been devised for representing a large number of spoken languages. Three types of writing (picture, ideographic, and alphabetic) represent the English words or concepts *car, carp,* and *carpet* in Figure 1–1.

The picture and ideographic writing are purely arbitrary. The ideographs are not taken from an established language. The most important feature of the ideographic writing is that there are no common features in the three symbols. The alphabetic writing is also arbitrary, but it is based on the alphabetic principle: the letter symbols and their order of occurrence have been universally agreed upon since they are taken from English writing. The first three letter symbols in each word are identical. They signal the reader to blend the same three speech sounds (phonemes) if the goal is to arrive

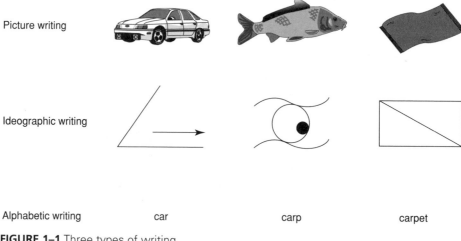

Picture writing

Ideographic writing

Alphabetic writing   car   carp   carpet

FIGURE 1–1 Three types of writing

at the spoken word that the various letter configurations represent. In the case of *carp* and *carpet,* the reader must blend still other phonemes.

There are many other spoken words in which one hears the same three phonemes in the same sequence. The graphic representation of these speech sounds will be the same in a number of printed words: *carnival, cardinal, card, cartoon.* In English writing, however, one may see the graphic symbols *car* and find that they represent different phonemes from the ones under discussion (*carol, care, career, caress, caret*).

Cracking the code. This term is generally used to describe the process of learning to associate printed letters with the speech sounds they represent. In a discussion of beginning reading, cracking the code refers to learning letter-sound relationships via the ability to apply phonics. When a child has learned to associate all of the specific printed letters with specific speech sounds, the code has been mastered, or cracked. The child now can arrive at or approximate the pronunciation of most printed word symbols.

Digraph. A digraph is a combination of two letters that represent one speech sound (consonant examples: *ch*urch, *sh*ow, *th*ank; vowel examples: b*ee*t, c*oa*t, m*ai*l).

Diphthong. A diphthong is a vowel blend: two adjacent vowels, each of which is sounded (*ou* in h*ou*se, *oi* in *oi*l, *oy* in b*oy,* *ow* in h*ow*).

Grapheme. A grapheme is a written or printed letter symbol used to represent a speech sound or phoneme.

Grapheme-phoneme relationship. This term refers to the relationship between printed letters and the sounds they represent; it also covers the deviations found in such a relationship. Thus, while English writing is based on an alphabetic code, there is not a one-to-one relationship between graphemes (printed symbols) and the phonemes (speech sounds) they represent. Some printed symbols represent several different sounds (*car, caress, cake*), and one speech sound may be represented by many different letters or combinations of letters (which we will discuss later in this chapter). To a great extent, this problem stems from the spelling patterns of words that have become established in English writing.

Morphemes. These are the smallest meaningful units of language. The word *cat* is a morpheme whose pronunciation consists of three phonemes. If one wishes to speak of more than one cat, the letter *s* forming the plural *cats* becomes a morpheme, since it changes the meaning (as does the possessive *'s* in the *cat's dinner*).

There are two classes of morphemes, free and bound. The former functions independently in any utterance (*house, lock, man, want*). Bound morphemes consist of prefixes, suffixes, and inflectional endings and must combine with other morphemes (house*s,* *un*lock, man*'s,* want*ed*).

Onset. An initial consonant or consonant cluster is an onset. In the word *name, n* is the onset; in the word *blame, bl* is the onset.

Phoneme. A phoneme is the smallest unit of sound in a language that distinguishes one word from another. Pronouncing the word *cat* involves blending three phonemes: /k/ /æ/ /t/.

Phonemic awareness. This term refers to the knowledge or understanding that speech consists of a series of sounds and that individual words can be divided into phonemes.

Phonetic method. This is a vague term that once was used to indicate instruction that included phonics, emphasized phonics, or overemphasized phonics. Eventually it acquired the polar connotation of "pro-phonics" and "anti-sight-word method." (We will discuss this dichotomy in Chapter 2.)

Phonetics. This term refers to the segment of linguistic science that deals with (a) speech sounds; (b) how these sounds are made vocally; (c) sound changes that develop in languages; and (d) the relation of speech sounds to the total language process. All phonics instruction is derived from phonetics, but phonics as it relates to reading utilizes only a relatively small portion of the body of knowledge identified as phonetics.

Phonic analysis. This is the process of applying knowledge of letter-sound relationships, that is, blending the sounds represented by letters so as to arrive at the pronunciation of printed words.

Phonics instruction. Phonics instruction is a facet of reading instruction that (a) leads the child to understand that printed letters in printed words represent the speech sounds heard when words are pronounced; and (b) involves the actual teaching of which sound is associated with a particular letter or combination of letters.

Rime. A rime is the vowel or vowel and consonant(s) that follow the onset. In the word *name, ame* is the rime.

Schwa. The schwa sound is a diminished stress, or a softening of the vowel sound. Schwa is represented by the symbol ə (bedlam = bed ləm; beckon = bek'ən). Any of the vowels may represent the schwa sound.

Sight vocabulary. A sight vocabulary includes any words a reader recognizes instantly, without having to resort to any word-recognition strategies.

Sight-word method. The term *sight-word method* is an abstraction rather than a description of reading instruction. Some beginning reading materials developed in the first half of the century, however, advocated teaching a limited number of sight words before phonic analysis was introduced. The term *sight-word method* became common even though it actually described only this initial teaching procedure. Gradually the term was used to imply the existence of an instructional approach that allegedly proscribed phonics and advocated teaching every new word by sight only.

Word analysis. This is an inclusive term that refers to all methods of word recognition. Phonics is one such method.

Limitations of Phonics

Phonics instruction does have limitations. Knowing this fact helps us avoid expecting too much of our lessons. It also helps us see why children need other related word recognition skills.

VARIABILITY OF LETTER-SOUNDS IN ENGLISH

The greatest limitation of the use of phonics is the spelling patterns of many English words. Although written English is alphabetic, the irregular spellings of words prevent anything like a one-to-one relationship between letters seen and sounds heard. Some of the reasons for, and examples of, this problem include the following:

1. Many English words have come from other languages such as Latin, Greek, French, and German (*waive, alias, corps, debris, alien, buoy, feint, bouquet*). The spelling of these words is often confusing.
2. A given letter, or letters, may represent different sounds in different words: *cow* = ow, *low* = ō; *can* = ă, *cane* = ā, *cap* = k, *city* = s; *bus* = s, *his* = z, *measure* = zh.
3. The following illustrate some of the variability found in English words. Some words (homonyms) are (a) pronounced the same, (b) spelled differently, and (c) each is phonetically "lawful":

weak—week	meat—meet	heal—heel	beat—beet
peal—peel	real—reel	peak—peek	steal—steel

In these examples, the generalization that applies to both spellings is *when there are two adjacent vowels in a word, usually the first is long and the second is not sounded.*

One word in each of the following pairs is governed by this phonic generalization; the other is not:

vain	rain	peace	wait
vein	reign	piece	weight

4. In hundreds of English words a letter or letters may represent no sound:

night	comb	often	wrong

5. A word may have one or more letters not sounded that differentiate it from another word pronounced exactly the same:

new	our	plum	cent	no
knew	hour	plumb	scent	know

6. The long sound of vowels may be represented by any of these and other combinations in words:

	day	they	fate	sail	reign	great
ā =	ay	ey	a(e)	ai	ei	ea
	feet	meat	deceive	brief	ski	key
ē =	ee	ea	ei	ie	i	ey
	my	kite	pie	height	buy	guide
ī =	y	i(e)	ie	ei	uy	ui

	show	hold	boat	note	go	sew
ō =	ow	o(+ ld)	oa	o(e)	o	ew
	flew	view	tube	due	suit	you
ū =	ew	iew	u	ue	ui	ou

One of the problems in teaching letter-sound relationships is that dozens of "rules" or "generalizations" have been developed to help learners arrive at the pronunciation of words they do not recognize. The following discussion focuses on three of the most widely used generalizations and their limited efficacy resulting from numerous exceptions.

1. *When two vowels are side by side in a word, the first usually has its long sound and the second is not sounded.*

Rule applies: boat, rain, meat, week, soap, sail, need
Exceptions: been, said, chief, dead, field, head, their

2. *When a word has two vowels, the second being final* e, *the first usually has its long sound and the final* e *is not sounded.*

Rule applies: ride, pale, hate, bite, dime, hide, cane, cute
Exceptions: love, done, have, come, give, none, once

3. *A single vowel in medial position in a word or syllable usually has its short sound.*

Extensive research has shown that the first two rules apply less than fifty percent of the time in high-frequency words. The third generalization can be useful to children learning to read. It applies to enough high-frequency words to justify calling it to students' attention. However, there is no phonetic rule that will apply to all words that meet the criteria the rule sets forth. The following illustrates how, when a rule does not apply to a number of words, a new rule emerges to cover this situation.

Exception A: *hold, cold, bold, gold; bolt, colt*
New rule: The single vowel o, followed by *ld* or *lt,* has its long sound.

Exception B: *car, fir, fur, her, for, part, bird, hurt, perch, corn*
New rule: A vowel followed by *r* has neither its long nor short sound—the vowel sound is modified by the *r.*

Exception C: *wild, mild, child; find, kind, mind, blind*
New rule: The vowel *i* before *ld* or *nd* is usually long.

Exception D: *fall, call, ball; salt, malt, halt*
New rule: The vowel *a* followed by *ll* or *lt* is pronounced like *aw* (ball = bawl).

Exception E: *high, sigh; light, night, bright, flight*
New rule: The vowel *i* in *igh* and *ight* words is usually long.

Other exceptions: sign = (i); was = (u); both = (ō); front = (u)

These examples deal only with monosyllabic words containing a single vowel in a medial position. There are also a number of consonant irregularities, discussed in chapter 5, but none of these represent the large number of sounding options that are characteristic of vowels. The "exceptions" to the basic rule are only the major ones that might logically be dealt with in teaching reading, and the words listed represent only a small fraction of those that could be cited. As rules become more involved and cover fewer and fewer actual words, one might question the relationship between learning these rules and learning the process called reading.

In recent years, teachers have had considerable data available that focus on the frequency with which various phonic rules apply to words children will meet in their primary and elementary school experiences. Studies by Oaks (1952), Clymer (1962), Bailey (1967), Emans (1967), Burmeister (1968), and Burrows and Lourie (1963) are in agreement in their findings that there are a significant number of exceptions to generalizations covering vowel sounds.

The educational issue is not arriving at a universally agreed upon list of rules to be taught. The real problem, which is much more complicated, is what happens to learners under various types of instruction that focus on rules. What types of attack strategies do children develop? There is little information to guide teachers. Those who have worked extensively with impaired readers have undoubtedly encountered some children who are rule oriented. Some of these children persist in trying to make the rule fit even when the word they are attacking is an exception. Others can cite the rule and still are unable to apply it to words that it covers.

Despite the absence of data that might serve as a guide for teaching phonic generalizations, teachers must decide on the teaching strategies they will use. They may choose instructional materials that make a fetish of memorizing phonic generalizations. They might, on the other hand, present a series of words governed by a particular rule and invite children to formulate a generalization. The latter course seems preferable, not just because it fits under the rubric *discovery method,* but because it permits children to work with concepts they can understand. Furthermore, it relieves the learning situation of a certain degree of rigidity and reduces the finality that is usually associated with a rule.

PHONICS: HISTORY AND CONTROVERSY

America is in the latter stages of repealing the dream of universal free education and the goal of educating all children to the maximum of their ability. Neither educators nor their critics believe the schools can educate all of the children that our society delivers to the schools. For decades criticism of American education has focused on reading, or more precisely, on the phonics component of that instruction.

Should educators, and specifically reading teachers, be conversant with past instructional methods and materials? It might be difficult to establish that knowledge of this history is essential for successful teaching of reading. However, such knowledge can be helpful in understanding some of the problems, attitudes, and misunderstandings that have been and still are associated with American reading instruction. The instructional programs and philosophies presented in the following discussion—both for and against phonics—were all devised by adults, allegedly with the best interests of children in mind. However, hindsight suggests the danger of permitting the beliefs of single-minded crusaders to go unchallenged.

EARLY TRENDS

During the latter part of the nineteenth century, beginning reading instruction stressed the teaching of the ABCs. Children were taught to recite the names of the letters that made up unknown words met in reading. It was believed that letter naming would provide the necessary phonetic clues for arriving at the spoken word the printed symbols represented. In essence, this was a spelling approach, since letter names often have little resemblance to speech sounds represented by letters (*come* = *see oh em ee* = *kum*). This approach, abandoned because it didn't work, was revived in 1961 by Leonard Bloomfield.

Prior to 1900, and continuing for over a decade, emphasis shifted from drill on letter names to drill on the sounds of the various letters. Rebecca Pollard's *Synthetic Method,* introduced in 1889, advocated reducing reading to a number of mechanical procedures, each of which focused on a unit smaller than a word. Reading became very mechanistic and, when mastered, often produced individuals who were adept at working their way through a given word. The result among both teachers and pupils was that reading became equated with "facility in calling words." A few of the recommended procedures of this method include the following:

1. Drills in articulation were to precede any attempt at reading. The child was to drill on the "sounds of letters." Then the child would be able, it was reasoned, to attack whole words.
2. Single consonants were "sounded." Each consonant was given a sound equivalent to a syllable. Thus, *b, c, d, p, h,* and *t* were sounded *buh, cuh, duh, puh, huh,* and *tuh.*
3. Drills on word families were stressed, without regard for word meanings. Sometimes children memorized lists of words ending in such common family phonograms as *ill, am, ick, ate, old,* and *ack.*
4. Diacritical markings were introduced in first grade, and children drilled on "marking sentences." For example: The ghŏst wăs a cŏmmŏn sīght near the wrĕck. He knew the īsland was ĕmpty.

This and similar approaches had a number of weaknesses including the following:

1. The sounds assigned to consonant letters were arbitrary.
2. Letter sounds were overemphasized and taught in isolation (*buh-ah-tuh = bat*).
3. This was true also as drill on vowel letter sounds was combined with initial consonant sounds (*ba, da, ha, ma, pa, ra,* etc.).
4. Drill instruction was not related to actual words or to actual reading.

It is easy to see that <u>this type of instruction placed little emphasis on reading as a meaning-making process. As children performed these ritualistic drills, they developed an inappropriate concept of reading that negatively influenced their reading beh</u>avior.

While these so called phonics instructional practices were indefensible, the response to these excesses was equally unrealistic. The revolt against the say-the-letters-ignore-the-meaning era resulted in behavior that seemed to suggest that children might learn to read if *words* were bypassed and instruction began immediately with larger units of print. These were called "meaning-bearing units," and it was suggested that beginning instruction focus on sentences, stories, and real literature.

In the book *American Reading Instruction (1934),* Nila B. Smith describes this period. Her book is the source for the several publications cited in the following brief discussion.

In 1895, George L. Farham published *The Sentence Method of Teaching Reading* (cited in Smith, 1934, p. 140). This approach advocated using whole sentences or even stories as a starting point. The teacher would read these "whole messages" to the class and repeat them many times. The children would then recite the material several times. The goal was to have children learn these passages. If they were successful, these activities were somehow equated with reading. Children were not taught to identify any of the words, except perhaps by their visual patterns. Thus, nothing they learned could transfer to the next reading experience if other words were involved. This approach became more aptly named when Charles McMurray, in 1897, published *The Method of Recitation* (cited in Smith, 1934, p. 117).

When support for the sentence-and-story-recitation methods waned, there emerged a movement to use literature as the reading curriculum. A number of reading textbooks published in this era are cited by Smith (1934, p. 122):

Stepping Stones to Literature (1897)

Graded Literature Series (1899)

Special Methods in Reading of Complete English Classics (1899)

In the latter text it was suggested that materials such as *Snow Bound, The Great Stone Face,* and *Julius Caesar* be read and studied as complete works. In agreement, Charles W. Eliot, then president of Harvard University, suggested that existing reading textbooks be removed because they were not *real* literature, just excerpts from literature. Smith (1934) wrote, "We found that between the approximate dates of 1880 and 1918 educators considered the supreme function of reading instruction to be that of developing appreciation for and permanent interest in literature" (p. 185).

The era of literature emphasis just sketched had an elitist component. This reading curriculum might possibly have made sense for that minority of young people destined for more advanced education, college, and the professions. The socioeconomic status of this group was a guarantee that they would acquire (in or out of school) the prerequisite of actually knowing how to read. The problem was that the majority of children in the public schools were not learning reading skills adequate to follow the literature curriculum.

REALITY CHECK: BASAL PROGRAMS

There were a number of changes taking place in American society that raised serious questions about the utility of literature as the reading curriculum. Compulsory education laws kept children in school longer, and students' inability to read caused the schools problems. Also, the workplace was demanding a higher level of literacy. Thus, the inability to read was noticed and became an issue in both the school and the larger community.

The result was a challenge to the magnificent obsession that exposure to literature (sans reading ability) could result in students reading literature. The alternative was to be to teach children to read—then teach the literature. Instruction would have to change. It would be slower, more obvious, more direct. Actual teaching materials could not continue to be adult-critiqued literature. To borrow a future criticism, there had to be a "dumbing down" of the reading curriculum.

This was accomplished with the emergence of a new wave of basal reading materials. Graded materials for primary-level instruction (grades 1–6) had been available for more than a century. However, these new materials were definitely a break with tradition. The chief difference was the dual thrust of reading textbooks accompanied by increased emphasis on workbooks that emphasized, taught, and reviewed reading skills. Several characteristics of these materials should be noted:

1. The difficulty level of the reading materials was held to an absolute minimum by severely controlling and limiting the introduction of printed words. After months of instruction, children were still dealing with stories limited to a vocabulary of 60 to 80 words.

2. This very limited vocabulary necessitated interminable repetition of words in the text materials. This was deadly for students, teachers, parents, and society. Nevertheless, the basals remained the materials of choice for several decades.

3. Basal programs were able to temporarily avoid entanglement in the polar positions regarding teaching phonics. There is no evidence of a deliberate effort to foster the appearance of neutrality in regard to phonics instruction. However, the actual reading textbooks contained little or no overt teaching of letter-sound relationships, while the workbook segments of the programs taught and reviewed phonics skills at every level. Thus, whatever position one preferred in regard to teaching phonics could be accommodated by how one chose to use and emphasize various parts of these programs.

Teachers were poorly served by this laissez-faire attitude toward phonics. There was little guidance in regard to the introduction, emphasis, or methodology involved in teaching phonics. For some teachers this instruction became less deliberate and less systematic. Many children experienced difficulty in becoming independent readers. In other classrooms, the workbooks became a substitute for teaching. There, mindless repetition of seatwork posing as reading turned children away from reading.

Teacher indecision about instructional practices left fertile ground for the reemergence of an old idea. During the 1850s and later, the conventional wisdom had been that beginning reading instruction should focus on children learning to recognize whole words. This practice could lead to success for a limited time. Children could learn to differentiate among a number of words relying on visual cues only. However, progress in learning broke down when children started to meet an avalanche of unknown words that were very similar in their visual patterns. The word method then gave way to the sentence method and the literature emphasis mentioned previously. The ambivalent attitude toward phonics instruction opened the door to a new version of the whole-word approach.

Sight-word Method
versus Phonetic Method

Gradually, the conventional wisdom decreed that children should learn a number of sight words prior to receiving any phonics instruction. This philosophy, then reflected in many of the basal materials that were used in the schools, had a tendency to delay phonics instruction. Somehow this instructional philosophy became labeled the "sight-word method."

It is probably safe to surmise that the term *sight-word method* led some people to believe that there was such a method. Since the term omits any reference to phonics, some people might have inferred that phonics was meant to be excluded. At the other end of the continuum, the same type of illogical labeling was taking place. A belief that letter-sound relationships should be taught made one an advocate of the *phonetic method.* Gradually, these two terms took on an either-or connotation, and these were the only positions available. One was either pro-phonics and opposed to teaching sight words or vice versa.

Although these labels could not, and did not, describe any instructional programs in the schools, they completely dominated the debate on reading instruction. Hundreds of research articles, most of them of dubious quality, divided quite evenly on espousing either the phonetic or sight-word method. Thus, the 20-year period preceding the 1950s did not witness any significant modifications in either instructional materials or methodology. All of the widely used basal reading programs were quite similar.

During this period, some children learned to read, some were definitely impaired readers, and very few loved to read. At reading conferences and conventions, teachers constantly asked, "How do you motivate children to read?" This question persisted because it never received a serious answer. There was no responsible answer as long as the then-existing reading curriculum was in place. Children were being asked to read bland, unchildlike materials while instruction moved them much too slowly toward becoming independent readers. Few suspected that things were about to get worse.

CRITICISM LEADS TO NEW PHONICS MATERIALS

As criticism of children's reading ability increased, hostility to existing instructional materials mounted. During the 1950s there were more focus and debate on reading instruction, and more demand and calls for change than there had been in any previous period. The major catalyst for change was a book written with the fervor that only a true believer could muster: In 1955, Rudolph Flesch published the book *Why Johnny Can't Read*.

Flesch's book came on the scene at exactly the right time. It was simplistic, but written with enough unabashed authority that it was hailed as a panacea. *Why Johnny Can't Read* was one dimensional in that lack of phonics instruction was the alleged problem, and more phonics was the only acceptable solution. There was, he claimed, a conspiracy within the reading establishment to prevent the teaching of phonics. Institutions involved with teacher preparation were a part of, and a moving force behind, this conspiracy. Having identified the problem, Flesch (1955) advanced a solution: Teach phonics my way and there will be no failures in learning to read. This publication eventually triggered a strong swing of the pendulum back to phonics instruction.

While Flesch was instrumental in arousing interest in phonics, his suggestions relative to teaching were quite primitive. His material consisted mostly of lists of words presenting different letter-sound patterns. Drill on these word lists was the extent of his instructional program. It was impossible for teachers to use these lists as a basis for instruction.

However, this instructional vacuum was soon filled with a number of new methods and materials that were developed and vigorously promoted. A number of supplementary "phonics emphasis" materials such as flash cards, workbooks, and tape recordings were offered as add-ons for any existing programs. In addition, whole new instructional programs with their own teaching materials were developed, including *Programmed Reading* (n.d.), *Words in Color* (1962), and the *Initial Teaching Alphabet* (ITA) (1963).

This new emphasis on code-cracking (phonics instruction) also spawned a set of instructional materials that were alleged to focus on cracking the code. However, their main thrust was total opposition to teaching any real phonics or letter-sound relationships. To illustrate the scope, philosophy, and inherent weaknesses of these new programs, two will be briefly summarized here. These are the *ITA,* which represented a strong phonics emphasis; and the *Linguistic Regular Spelling* program, which proscribed the teaching of phonics.

THE INITIAL TEACHING ALPHABET (ITA)

The Initial Teaching Alphabet was developed in England by Sir James Pitman in order to achieve a more uniform letter-seen–sound-heard relationship in English writing. This was first called the Augmented Roman Alphabet, since it consisted of 44 rather than 26 letter symbols (Figure 2–1).

The use of 44 symbols permits a much closer approximation of a one-to-one relationship between printed letters and the sounds they represent. Obviously, teaching with the ITA involved the development and use of reading materials printed in the ITA.

FIGURE 2–1 Pitman's Initial Teaching Alphabet (ITA)

Source: From Richard Fink and Patricia Keiserman, ITA Teacher Training Workbook and Guide (New York: Initial Teaching Alphabet Publications, 1969). Reprinted by permission.

Since the materials were concerned only with initial instruction, learners had to transfer from the ITA materials to materials printed in regular orthography sometime near the end of first grade.

The ITA Instructional Program

The ITA involved more than just the use of a modified orthography. Several salient instructional features were an integral part of its methodology:

1. Children were not taught letter names, but they were taught that each ITA symbol represented a particular sound. Early instruction consisted of systematic teaching of these symbol-sound relationships.
2. From the very beginning of instruction, children were taught to write using the ITA symbols. Writing, which involves spelling of words, reinforced the phonics instruction (letter-sound relationships).
3. In ITA instruction, children learned only the lowercase letters. Capitals were indicated simply by making the letter larger. Thus, the child did not have to deal with two different symbols for the same letter (A a, B b, C c, D d, E e, F f, G g, H h) in the initial stages of learning to read and write. In essence, what this practice did was to delay for a time the child's need to master both sets of symbols.
4. Promotional materials for the ITA claimed that there was a high degree of compatibility between ITA and traditional spellings. A fact ignored was that ITA materials frequently resorted to phonetic respelling of irregularly spelled words.

ITA: Postponing the Difficult

As the title *Initial Teaching Alphabet* implies, this was an approach that focused on beginning reading only. Beginning reading tasks were simplified in several ways:

1. Capital letter forms were not introduced.
2. Irregularly spelled words were respelled.
3. All long vowel sounds were represented by two adjacent vowel letters.

Particular attention had to be paid to the various respellings, which resulted in a high degree of consistency between letters seen and sounds heard. This would have had great virtue if it had represented a real spelling reform. However, at the time of transfer, children had to face the reality of irregular spellings while having been taught that words could be sounded by blending the sounds of the letters seen. This mind set that was developed during initial teaching could easily inhibit growth when irregular spellings were met in great profusion in traditional orthography. Table 2–1 illustrates respellings that have nothing to do with the modified alphabet.

Some of these respellings change the visual pattern of words quite drastically, which does not facilitate transfer to traditional print and spelling. While this practice might have resulted in a rapid start in beginning reading, it had minimal effects on children cracking the main code. They eventually had to deal with irregular words when they transferred to traditional orthography.

In addition to the phonetic respellings, which did not involve any of the new ITA characters, many spelling changes involved a reshuffling of vowels. The vowel changes

TABLE 2–1 *Initial Teaching Alphabet* Respellings

enough – – – – – enuf	anyone – – – – enywun	said – – – – – – – sed
once – – – – – – – wuns	large – – – – – larj	next – – – – – – – nekst
lovely – – – – – – luvly	many – – – – – meny	George – – – – – – Jorj
crossed – – – – – crosst	some – – – – – sum	one – – – – – – – wun
six – – – – – – – siks	money – – – – muny	couple – – – – – – cupl
glove – – – – – – gluv	laugh – – – – – laf	none – – – – – – – nun
wax – – – – – – – waks	ought – – – – aut	someone – – – – – sumwun
yacht – – – – – – yot	tough – – – – tuf	trouble – – – – – – trubl

TABLE 2–2 *Initial Teaching Alphabet* Two-vowel generalization

also – – – – – – – auls œ	night – – – – – nıet	find – – – – – – – f ınd
their – – – – – – thær	so – – – – – – – s œ	seized – – – – – – s ee zd
there – – – – – – thær	idea – – – – – ı d ee a	wife – – – – – – – w ıe f
I – – – – – – – – ı	most – – – – – mœst	walked – – – – – – w au kt
knows – – – – – n œs	came – – – – – c æm	ate – – – – – – – æt
fire – – – – – – – fıe r	lace – – – – – l æ s	owe – – – – – – – œ
my – – – – – – – m ıe	phone – – – – f œ n	page – – – – – – – pæj
sight – – – – – – sıe t	weight – – – – w æ t	gave – – – – – – – g æ v
giant – – – – – j ıe ant	nice – – – – – n ıe s	people – – – – – – p ee pl
eyes – – – – – – ıe s	five – – – – – f ıe v	life – – – – – – – l ıe f

and transpositions were made so that the spelling would follow the "two-vowel generalization": when two vowels come together, the first has its long sound and the second is silent. Some examples of this are presented in Table 2–2.

Transfer from the ITA to Traditional Orthography

Concurrently with the introduction and use of the ITA in America, there were assurances from many quarters that transfer from the ITA to traditional print would not pose a problem. This optimism was allegedly grounded on reports from England. While John Downing of England was actively promoting the experimental use of the ITA in America, his 1963 publication, *Experiments with Pitman's Initial Teaching Alphabet in British Schools,* contained a note of caution on the issue of transfer:

> If teachers *opinions* [italics added] are supported by the results of the objective tests conducted last month [March 1963], we may feel encouraged in *our hopes* [italics added] that all children will pass through the transfer stage with success, but *we must urge the greatest caution in drawing final conclusions or taking action on the basis of this preliminary trial.* [italics added] (p. 125)

Downing's caution was vindicated by the outcome of studies in England and America. In the December 1967 issue of *Elementary English,* Downing stated,

Although teachers' subjective impressions of the transition stage have suggested that it is smooth and effortless, test results show that i.t.a. students from about mid-second year until about mid-third year do not read t.o. [traditional orthography] as well as they read i.t.a. a few weeks or even months previously. . . . More specifically, the British experiments show that children are not transferring from i.t.a. to t.o. in quite the way originally predicted. (p. 849)

Reading achievement resulting from the use of the ITA failed to establish this medium as superior to traditionally printed materials *in which methodology also stressed systematic phonics instruction.*

THE LINGUISTIC (REGULAR SPELLING) APPROACH

Of all the newer methods that emerged in the post-Flesch period, this one may well be the strangest. These materials were first published by Leonard Bloomfield in 1942. For the next decade Bloomfield and his colleague Clarence L. Barnhart collaborated in efforts to have the materials adapted and used in mainstream reading instruction. However, during this time they received little if any favorable response or acceptance.

After Bloomfield's death and the increasing emphasis on teaching phonics, Barnhart published *Let's Read: A Linguistic Approach* in 1961. The materials contained therein had no roots in any branch of linguistic science. However, Bloomfield was a noted linguist and the term *linguistics* was popular and frequently invoked by critics of reading instruction. Thus the subtitle *A Linguistic Approach.*

The irony of *Let's Read* is that it was published as part of the *Why Johnny Can't Read* revolution, the main thrust of which was the relentless, hard-nosed teaching of phonics or code cracking. Somehow, *Let's Read* was able to pose as code-cracking material even though the teaching of phonics or letter-sound relationships was proscribed.

The most tenable hypothesis as to how this could have happened was that the material so closely resembled a previously used phonics instructional approach that the two were confused. This was especially the case in regard to the systematic teaching of a series of words that each ended with the same phonogram. This was called the "word-family" approach, and the word families were identical to the spelling patterns stressed in the regular spelling approach. Some examples are *cat, hat, mat, fat, bat* and *can, man, tan, fan, ran.* The teaching methodologies involved in the two approaches, however, were antithetical. In the word-family method, children were taught to think and say the sound represented by the first letter. This sounding clue helped them distinguish between the sounds of the words c*at,* h*at,* m*at,* f*at,* b*at,* s*at,* p*at,* and r*at.* In the regular spelling methodology, children had to learn each word configuration by memory.

The Regular Spelling Instructional Program

Vocabulary control (regular spelling concept). The major premise of these materials was that initial instruction should be based exclusively on a unique vocabulary-control principle. This principle was that in early reading instruction, the child should meet only those words that have "regular spellings," a term used to designate words in which printed letters represent "the most characteristic sound" associated with each letter.

The word *cat* would meet this criterion, but the word *cent* would be irregular because the *c* does not represent the characteristic *k* sound but rather the sound usually represented by *s*. The spelling of *bird* is irregular because the *i* represents a sound usually represented by *u* (burd) as does the *o* in *come* (kum).

Initial teaching (letter names, not letter sounds). In the regular spelling approach, the child was taught letter recognition and letter names (aye, bee, see, dee, ee, eff). After the letters are learned in isolation they are combined into words:

> The child need not even be told that the combinations are words; and he should certainly not be required to recognize or read words. *All he needs to do is read off the names of the successive letters, from left to right.* [italics added] (Bloomfield, 1961, p. 36)

Then the child is ready to begin working his way through a series of words that end with identical letter-phoneme patterns (*can, fan, man, tan*). Bloomfield (1961) suggested that teaching should proceed as follows:

1. Print and point to the word CAN.
2. The child is to read the letters "see aye en."
3. The teacher states "now we have spelled the word. Now we are going to *read* it. This word is can. Read it *can*."
4. Present another word from the "an family" such as tan. (p. 41)

The aim of this teaching method was to have the child distinguish between various words that differ only in the initial grapheme-phoneme. However, the child was never taught the association between the initial letter and the sound it represents in words. There is no question but that a child must learn this relationship in order to become an independent reader.

 Meaning waived in beginning instruction. Unfortunately, many of the English words we use most frequently in building even the simplest of sentences have irregular spellings. Some examples include *a, the, was, once, of, any, could, love, too, their, do, said, one, who, some, only, gone, live, father, give, many, are, would, come, head, both, again, been, have, they, there, to, get,* and *should*. Typical English sentences are difficult to build when one decides to use only words that follow regular spelling patterns. For example, in Bloomfield's (1961) material, after the teaching of 66 words (roughly equivalent to several preprimers in a representative basal series), one finds only the most contrived sentences and absolutely no story line:

> Pat had ham.
> Nat had jam.
> Sam had a cap.
> Dan had a hat.
> Sam ran.
> Can Sam tag Pam?
> Can Pam tag Sam? (p. 65)

no natural language

After 200 words had been learned, the child read these sentences:

Let Dan bat.
Did Al get wet?
Van had a pet cat.
Get up, Tad!
Let us in, Sis!
Sis, let us in!
Let Sid pet a pup. (Bloomfield, 1961, p. 87)

If letter-sound relationships were learned, the child could then use this learning in future reading tasks. For instance, learning the sound that *b* represents in the word b*at* would transfer to the *b* in other word families such as b*et,* b*it,* b*ut,* b*ad,* b*ud,* b*id,* b*ug,* b*un,* b*us,* b*ag,* b*ig,* and b*ed.* More important, the knowledge of the sound *b* represents would also function in words with irregular spellings because the sound represented by *b* remains consistent in hundreds of these words (barn, ball, bath, bird, bold, busy, burn, both, bow).

Only 38% of the *Let's Read* program consisted of regularly spelled words. It is clear that what was learned in the initial instruction was not expected to transfer to the remaining two thirds of the program. Bloomfield (1961) revealed the Achilles heel of the material when he stated,

"When it comes to teaching irregular and special words, each word will demand a separate effort and separate practice" (p. 206).

No guidelines or blueprint for such instruction was provided. Initial instruction soon exhausted the easier aspects of learning to read. Then children and teachers were abandoned when the more difficult aspects of learning to read could no longer be avoided.

THE INDIVIDUALIZED READING AND LANGUAGE EXPERIENCE APPROACHES

While the highly structured beginning reading programs just discussed were seeking converts, there also emerged a philosophy of reading instruction that sought to curtail or abolish much of the structure and routine associated with the basal programs. This new philosophy operated under the twin banner of the *Individualized Reading Movement* and the *Language Experience Approach.* The chief premises of these new approaches included the following:

1. Reliance on basal reader materials was to be avoided. These were considered to be too restrictive, dull, and uninspiring.
2. Trade books (children's literature) were to be plentiful in every classroom.
3. Children were to select the reading materials they wished to read.
4. Both reading and writing were to be incorporated into the reading instruction curriculum. They were considered to be complementary parts of language acquisition.
5. Children were to write, or dictate to the teacher, their own experiences or stories. These reading materials were to remain available in the classroom as long as the materials had motivational value.

6. Teachers were to schedule a time period for any child who could profit from a teacher-pupil conference.

7. Workbooks and their repetitive teaching of skills were frowned upon.

This new emphasis on children reading children's literature was a significant departure from the turn of the century's emphasis on literature. Then, the focus had been on adult classics that had been authenticated by adults as having "cultural value." The emphasis on children's literature as an integral part of the reading-instruction curriculum was a significant development. This was a reform that contained the potential for an educational revolution.

WHOLE LANGUAGE

The individualized reading approach's break with traditional instruction and its emphasis on integrating writing and reading instruction became the foundation for the whole-language movement. Whole language is not an instructional program, and its proponents do not claim that it is. It has been called a philosophy, a dynamic system of beliefs, a child-centered curriculum, and a means for empowering children. Goodman (1992), describing the status of whole language, writes, "Whole language is producing a holistic reading and writing curriculum which uses real authentic literature and real books" (p. 196).

Both supporters and critics agree that the concept of whole language is vague. One is invited into a seemingly attractive territory for which there is as yet no map. Its position is reminiscent of descriptions of individualized reading made in the mid-1970s:

> Paradoxically its greatest potential strengths and weaknesses stem from the same factor. There is no concise definition of "what it is" and thus no blueprint for 'how to do it'. . . . In one sense, individualized reading focuses on the child-as-a-reader more than the teacher-as-a-teacher. (Heilman, 1977, pp. 306–308)

Goodman (1992) has written that "whole language aims to be an inclusive philosophy of education" (p. 196). Actually, it has not been totally inclusive. There is a litmus test that proscribes the direct teaching of *reading skills* (which is a codeword for *phonics*). This cannot be explained away as being a gratuitous diversion: It is the chief article of faith of true believers in whole language. Whole language can fit comfortably at every level of the curriculum except for the period called "learning to read." Here one must develop the skills needed to move into a literature curriculum.

✦ Whole language is the latest version of that magnificent obsession that children might be successful in reading literature prior to solving the written code. What sustains this recurring dream? Is it based on the fact that learning the code is not a totally pleasant experience? Adult critics have noticed this as they observe children learning to read. When these adult, expert readers read, they are immersed in and sustained by the power and beauty of language. They say, "Let beginning reading be like this. Let beginning readers become involved with the beauty of language that resides in literature." To believe that this can occur, it is necessary to blur the difference between reading and learning to read. However, reading and learning to read are not synonymous. Learning to read is the price we pay in order to read literature.

Relative to this discussion, Jerome Bruner, a psychologist who helped develop the cognitive approach in the 1950s, made a significant observation and shared it with reading teachers. He said, "learning to read is not a self-sustaining activity" (1972). He knew that learning to read is not the same activity that expert readers experience when they read. For learners, some of the joy is missing. The power and beauty of language is held hostage by the unknown words that interrupt the melody of language.

While learning to read may not be a self-sustaining activity, it is an activity that must be sustained until children make it to the next level, which is reading. Readers, by definition, can deal independently with the printed page. Children at all levels of reading ability will meet some words that they do not instantly recognize. But if they have mastered the code, they will be able to solve the identity of most of these words. Once children reach this point on the learning-to-read continuum, they are ready for the whole-language curriculum.

3

PHONICS AND
READING INSTRUCTION

Educators often have difficulty convincing critics that learning to read and teaching read-ing are difficult and frustrating experiences. They listen as educators explain that read-ing is getting meaning, and they readily admit both that children come to school with a highly developed mastery of language including a vast array of meanings, and that dur-ing the first two years of reading instruction, children will not be asked to read material that contains concepts beyond their grasp. Then, when educators insist that the school must build on what the child brings to school, it appears that learning to read should be a snap. While reading is getting meaning, *learning to read* is much more!

Children can handle "What do these words mean?"

Their problem is "What are these words?"

The only solution is learning to identify words. To do this the child must learn the relationship between visual cues (letters) and the speech sounds they represent (phoneme-grapheme relationships). After words have been identified and have been met hundreds of times, they are recognized. These words are now known, and no process of identifying them is required. Getting to this stage is called "learning to read." Learning to read is a difficult task because learning letter-sound relationships is totally foreign to any of the child's previous experiences.

HOW CHILDREN LEARN TO READ

Learning to read is a complicated, long-term process. Few adults can recall significant details of how they learned to read. If we observe someone teaching a child to read, we are seeing a very small segment of instruction. Every observation would focus on the teaching of a particular skill. Observing the teacher, the materials, and the methodology, however, would not reveal what is taking place within the learner. If we observe the learner, we are limited to a number of overt behaviors from which we hy-pothesize what mental processes are at work.

Assume that on the first day of school, the first-grade teacher points to a word in a story and asks a nonreader, "What is this word?" Obviously, the child cannot answer. If the teacher says, "I will read you the sentence leaving out that word. Listen carefully and then tell me the word." She reads, "The teacher asked the new girl, 'What is your _____?' " Probably 95% of first-grade nonreaders could supply the missing word. This illustrates what nonreaders bring to school that relates to reading. Children are adequately equipped to deal with the language-meaning aspect of reading. But they cannot begin with the magic of language until they have established what words these strange symbols represent.

After a few weeks of "learning to read," the children will have changed drastically. For example, a child is reading a story that contains fewer than a dozen different words. The reader does not recognize the word *man* in the sentence, *The man is sad.* The teacher suggests, "Sound it out." The child instantly responds "Boy."

The peculiar thing about this situation is that the child heard the teacher and had the ability to do what was suggested. However, the child had already settled on a response that had worked before—guessing. In recent reading experiences, the child had met many words he did not instantly recognize and at various times had tried all the following responses:

- Skipping the word
- Asking someone for help (teacher, parent, or peer)
- Ignoring all phonic clues and guessing the word
  (bad guess; makes no sense; the child then sounds it out)
  (good guess; correct word; reinforces guessing)
- Applying phonics to sound out the word
- Sounding out the first letter and instantly guessing the word
  (saying the wrong word; it makes sense; no problem)
  (saying the wrong word; it makes sense; big problem, because this time the substitute word demands changes later in the paragraph in order to keep the meaning)
- Trying to apply phonics, which doesn't work on the irregularly spelled word *once;* the child falls back on context clues, and solves the word
- Ad infinitum . . .

It is apparent that the beginning reader has many available options for solving unknown words. Some of these are very poor responses, but unfortunately, even the poorest are reinforced occasionally. Learning to read involves discarding ineffective responses and using all available clues that make for success. To make reasonable progress, the beginning reader must acquire three closely related skills:

- Mastering and applying letter-sound relationships
- Enlarging sight vocabulary
- Profiting from context clues while reading

Beginning reading instruction is so important because it is during that time that children develop a sense of what reading is. It is not good instruction to devote the first few months of reading to one of the three necessary skills while ignoring the other two. This kind of approach will confuse a child regarding the true nature of the reading process. An extensive time block devoted to phonics instruction leads the child to view reading as sounding out words. On the other hand, a lengthy instructional period without insight into letter-sound relationships leads a child to see reading as a process in which you guess at words you don't know. Serious damage to the learner can result from either approach. Early instruction should help learners develop the insight that these three skills complement each other in helping to crack the two codes—word identification and meaning. The only way children can miss the fact that reading is a meaning-making process is to receive instruction that masks this fact.

Obviously essential to reading is cracking the code, or learning to associate printed letters with the speech sounds they represent. Everything in spoken English can be printed using only 26 different letter symbols. This is possible because, in general, letters and letter combinations stand for the same speech sounds in thousands of different words. Despite the fact that there is not a one-to-one correspondence between letters seen and speech sounds represented, learning to read depends on mastery of the symbol-sound relationship.

To illustrate how phonics works, we will focus on what the child gains by learning one letter-sound relationship. (Teaching letter-sound relationships is discussed in later chapters.) Here we will simply assume that the child has been taught to do the following:

1. visually recognize the letter form *m,* and
2. associate *m* with the sound it represents at the beginning of words such as *man, my,* and *met.*

Of course, before coming to school, children have mastered several important related skills:

> They can make the *m* sound in hundreds of spoken words.
>
> They can differentiate this sound in all of the words (language) they hear. In listening to speech they do not confuse the word *man* with the words *can, pan, fan, ran,* or *tan*—even though the difference in the sounds of these words is minimal.

Phonics instruction invites the child to internalize the following in his own language:

> When I see the letter *m* I think of the sound it represents. This is the first sound in the familiar words, *me* and *my.*
>
> Any unknown word I meet that begins with *m* starts with the same sound as *me* and *my.*

The unknown word *man* cannot be b*oy,* c*at,* or g*irl;* or p*an,* r*an,* or f*an.* The correct word must begin like *me* and *my.* Next, teaching will focus on the sounds represented by medial vowels and final consonants. Each step mastered provides a bit more independence in reading.

The most frustrating aspect of teaching reading is that instruction cannot focus directly and exclusively on what children already know—the meanings imbedded in what they are asked to read. The intervening step of discovering the identity of the words is what complicates the procedures of learning to read. These procedures can take a lot of the joy out of learning. The problem stems from our reluctance to accept the fact that there is little in common between learning to read and skillful reading. The expert and the learner may be on the same learning continuum, but they are not engaged in the same activity.

Despite the difficulties in learning to read, there is no cause for despair. We must remember that when a child meets an unknown word, whatever it is that goes through her mind is handled much faster than any discussion of this phenomenon. Every gain a child makes in learning to read will transfer to future learning situations. For instance, after several weeks of instruction, she will have met some words so frequently that she will recognize them instantly. Once this happens she will never again puzzle over the speech sounds represented by individual letters in these words.

Soon the reader is able to deal with sentences and larger units of print. The fact that reading must follow the rules of speech is now a tremendous asset to the beginning reader. This is where the child is quite proficient; many reading "errors" become self-correcting. Instruction can now build on what the child knows. We will see how some specific learnings can inhibit growth while others provide insights and momentum in the learning-to-read process.

OVERVIEW OF WORD ANALYSIS SKILLS

We have already listed a number of responses that children might use when they read unknown words. In the literature on reading, these attempts to solve unknown words have been discussed as *word attack skills, word analysis skills,* or *word identification skills.* These are the major approaches one might use to identify unknown words:

- Unique letter or word configuration clues
- Picture clues
- Phonic analysis
- Structural analysis
- Context clues

Word Form (Unique Letter Configuration Clues)

This is the least useful of the various clues available for solving unknown words. It is doubtful that there is any value in teaching children to look for odd or striking visual letter patterns. It is probable, however, that some children will note certain of these on their own. In general, all words (except homographs: *wind-wind; lead-lead*) can be said to be unique in appearance. Yet, in the experience of a primary-level child, the visual forms of words are so much alike that much practice is needed to perceive the minute differences among them. While learning to discriminate word forms, the child might note such limited factors as the length of words or special features such as *tt, ll, oo,* or final *y.* Learning to recognize the word *monkey* because it has a tail (*y*) at the end may serve an immediate and limited purpose, but soon the child will meet *money, merry, funny,* and *penny.* The word *look* may be learned as having two eyes in the middle, but soon the child meets *book, stood,* and *flood.* It is obvious that, as the child expands his reading, these unique features are found in a large number of words and thus become of less and less value in identifying different words.

Picture Clues

Certain critics oppose the use of pictures in early reading materials on the basis that some children will rely too heavily on pictures; if this occurs, it interferes with learning to read. Those critical of using pictures often advocate approaches that emphasize code cracking in beginning reading. Materials of this nature do not usually lend themselves to very meaningful illustrations.

It is true that pictures may provide clues to unknown words (*turkey, cliff, wagon, father, bridge, fireplace*). Pictures may suggest words. In addition, they also have high motivational value and will often lure a child into reading. Pictures help focus attention on meaning; they lead into a story, and where only a limited number of words are known, pictures supplement. They serve as stimuli for oral language use in group discussions.

When children are observed to overrely on picture clues, this observation should have diagnostic significance for the teacher. It suggests that certain instructional practices may need closer examination, rather than that pictures should be proscribed in children's reading materials.

Phonic Analysis

Phonic analysis, or cracking the code, has been defined and discussed; here we will limit restatements to three sentences that summarize what it is, what it does, and what it isn't. Phonics instruction *is* teaching letter-sound relationships. Its *purpose* is to provide beginning readers with a means of identifying unknown printed words. Phonics *is not* a method of teaching reading, but it is an essential ingredient of reading instruction.

Structural Analysis

Structural analysis deals with one of the most important cue systems available to children learning to read. Root words are among the first words children learn (*look, call, fill, move, stop, need*). In English writing there are a large number of prefabricated, highly consistent spelling patterns that are added to thousands of root words; for example, prefixes such as *un-, re-, dis-, pre-, con-,* and *in-;* inflectional endings such as *-s, -ed,* and *-ing;* and suffixes such as *-ment, -tive, -ly, -less,* and *-able.*

Profiting from structural analysis instruction depends to some degree on previous learnings. If the child is familiar with the word *fill,* she may have little trouble identifying *re*fill, or even *re*fill*able,* even though affixes completely surround the root word. Beginning readers need to develop awareness of the visual changes produced in words by doing the following:

Adding affixes

Combining two words to form compounds (*anyone, somewhere*)

Writing plurals (*s-es-ies*)

Forming contractions (*can't, I'll, doesn't, I've*)

Context Clues

When a child is reading for meaning, the context in which he meets an unknown word is useful in suggesting what the word might be. Usually, only a few words could possibly fill out the meaning; for example:

The boy threw the ball to his _____.

Probably fewer than a dozen words could logically be inserted in the blank space (*friend, dog, mother, playmate, sister, father, brother*). Some possibilities would be less logical than others depending on what has happened in the story prior to this sentence.

Authors use a number of devices to provide context clues that help readers solve new words and difficult concepts. One of these is to incorporate a description-definition in the text:

They were now traveling through _____ country. It was very hot, there was sand underfoot, and the wind blew sand in their eyes. There were no streams—no water whatsoever—and no shade trees. The _____ extended as far as the eye could see.

Other techniques include comparison, contrast, and the use of synonyms and antonyms:

At this point the stream flowed very _____ [rapidly]. The water splashed over the rocks and sent up white spray as it moved swiftly through the pass.

Solving the identity of an unknown word is facilitated by (a) the meaning of the total sentence in which the word occurs, and (b) what has occurred in previously read sentences and sentences that follow—assuming, of course, that the child is reading for meaning.

SKILLS IN COMBINATION

The approaches to word analysis that we have described are not of equal value in learning to read. Different children may learn to rely on one method more than on others, and some approaches, such as unique word form, have limited utility beyond the early stages of learning to read. Facile reading would not result if one went through a series of trial-and-error responses using only one of the preceding approaches to word analysis. Efficient readers use various methods of word attack simultaneously.

Seeing phonics in proper perspective involves (a) understanding that phonic analysis is one means by which children can solve words not known as sight words; and (b) noting that phonics relates to, and interacts with, all the other methods of word analysis. For example, structural and phonic analysis constantly interact. Such prefabricated units as *ex-, pre-, dis-, en-, pro-, -ed, -ing, -tive, -ment,* and *-tion,* when added to words, do produce structural changes. Each of these, and many more, are also phonic units. The pronunciation of prefixes, suffixes, and compound words remains quite consistent.

Structural changes in a word will often camouflage clues the reader might have used in recognizing the root. When a child does not instantly recognize such a new word, she should resort to sounding. For example, a child may know the word *locate*, but not recognize *dislocated* or *relocating*. Sounding the parts will unlock the pronunciation and, since the meaning of the root word is known, the meaning of the new word is grasped. A child should not be taught to rely exclusively on one method or approach for solving unknown words. In the incomplete sentence under "Context Clues," we noted that the context permits several logical choices:

The boy threw the ball to his _____.

Here the reader is restricted to context alone. But with good instruction she will learn not to rely exclusively on context clues. In addition, in an actual reading situation she would not be confronted with a blank space, but rather a series of letters. Notice that when the reader heeds the initial letter and solves the sound it represents, the number of logical choices is drastically reduced:

The boy threw the ball to his s__ __ __ __ __.

It is doubtful the reader will need more than the minimal clue provided, but if the reader needs to, she may sound and blend more of the letters: sis__ __ __.

Context clues are not limited to the sentence in which the unknown word occurs. For example, assume a child is reading the following sentence in which the blank represents an unknown word:

"Look," said Jack, "look at the _____."

The context of this example alone does not provide enough context clues for the reader to solve the unknown word. In the following example, the sentence appears in a larger context:

"I hear a car," said Jack.
"I do not hear a car," said Suzy. "I hear a funny noise."
"I hear a honk-honk," said Jack, "but I do not see a car."
"That noise is in the sky," said Suzy.
Jack pointed at the sky. "Look," said Jack, "look at the g__ __ __ __ __."
Suzy said, "They are flying south for the winter."

At this point, some readers' background and previous experience will suggest the unknown word. The context suggests several classes of subjects, such as birds or airplanes, which would be logical. In the child's book, however, the unknown is not a blank space, but a word composed of letters. The sounds these letters represent have been studied. Even though the word is not known, the child who has been properly taught will note the initial consonant *g*. She will not say *bird* or *airplane* or any other word that does not begin with the *g* sound. She will sound as much as she needs:

Look at the g__ __ __ __ __.
gee__ __.
geese.

This story, because it is at the primary level, is accompanied by a picture that shows both children looking up, with Jack pointing toward the sky to a V-formation of geese. Thus, context, previous experience, a picture, sounding the initial consonant, then the double vowel, if needed, all provide clues to help the reader solve the unknown word without a noticeable hesitation. The less facile reader might require a pause in her reading while she sounds out the word. Only a very inefficient reader would have to depend entirely on "sounding out" every letter in the unknown word, which would involve wasting all the other clues.

INSTRUCTIONAL ISSUES IN PHONICS INSTRUCTION

Phonics instruction has always been surrounded by controversy, and past and present debate has failed to settle many of the issues. A few examples of questions raised over the years include: Are phonics skills essential for learning to read? If so, how much skill is needed? When should phonics instruction be introduced? In what sequence should skills be learned? Should children be taught phonics rules? Is phonics instruction an additive to beginning instruction or an integral part of it? What is the best methodology for teaching letter-sound relationships: Teaching sounds in isolation? Blending sounds in words? Using substitute alphabets? Diacritical marks? Whole-word regular spelling patterns? Programming the steps? Systematic or incidental instruction? Does phonics instruction produce slow readers who are unconcerned with meaning? Is the teaching of phonics and sight words compatible—or antithetical? Since expert readers can't be detected using phonics, why should beginners be burdened with it? Let us touch on a number of these instructional issues.

Is the Mastery of Phonics Skills Essential for Learning to Read?

This is really the issue that has nurtured the phonics vs. sight-word controversy for more than a century. The major premise of this book is that beginning readers who do not learn and apply the letter-sound code can progress only so far in learning to read. It would be futile to attempt to say exactly how far each child can go in terms of words he can learn in the absence of phonics skills. It is fairly safe to say, however, that no child will function as a fluent reader, or even as an average third-grade reader, if he does not learn to apply letter-sound relationships in his reading.

It is also safe to say that if a learner progresses in beginning reading without applying the letter-sound code, he will spend more time reading less material. The reason is obvious to the person who has worked with individuals who are learning to read. The terms *learning to read* and *beginning readers* imply limited experience with the written symbol system. The beginning reader faces the burden of making many visual discriminations among printed words that contain only minimal differences in visual cues. Unless letter-sound clues are added, the visual discrimination circuit overloads, and the reading process breaks down.

Why Teach Phonics in Beginning Reading?

Psycholinguists and other theorists have observed that expert readers rely very little, if at all, on letter-sound relationships. They obviously pay no heed to individual letters and cannot be observed applying phonics skills.

A potentially dangerous generalization is that since skilled readers do not appear to use phonics, perhaps children learning how to read need not be taught letter-sound relationships. If such a hypothesis is advanced, it should be accompanied by a description of how the learner will learn to read. One suggestion is that, possibly, memory for word forms (i.e., visual memory) may be all that is really needed. Smith (1973) writes:

> We can both recognize and recall many thousands of words in our spoken language vocabulary, and recognize many thousands of different faces and animals and plants and objects in our visual world. *Why should this fantastic memorizing capacity suddenly run out in the case of reading?* (p. 75)

Smith does not come out flatly against phonics instruction; however, the question he raises seems to invite the conclusion that visual memory of word configurations should be sufficient for learning to read. If this point of view gains adherents, we shall have come back full circle to the sight-word versus phonics debate. This debate should not be reopened without evidence that children can learn to read without applying letter-sound relationships in the beginning reading stage.

As we try to solve the mystery of how children learn to read, we must not observe experts and generalize from them to beginners. There are no experts who failed to learn and apply letter-sound relationships, and there are no experts who continue to use phonic clues as they did as beginners. Being expert readers precludes this behavior.

What Is the Optimum Amount of Phonics for a Given Child?

The optimum amount of phonics instruction a child should receive is the minimum amount she needs to become an independent reader. To provide less instruction than a child needs would deny her the opportunity to master a skill she must have to progress in independent reading. To subject children to drill they do not need runs the risk of destroying interest in the act of reading. It is easy to turn off a potential learner by requiring that she sit through group drill on sounding letters or complete a series of workbook pages that force her to deal with minute details of word attack when she is already capable of applying these skills in sustained reading.

The key to providing children with what they need in the way of instruction is knowledge of their weaknesses. We acquire this knowledge through diagnosis. The best diagnosis is observation and analysis of reading behavior. Discovering what a child needs in the area of code-cracking ability should be relatively easy, since she cannot help but disclose her needs. Every technique she might use to cover her weakness is an added clue.

When beginning readers omit, miscall, or substitute words, one tries to find out why. Miscues that do not distort meaning become of minor importance only after a child demonstrates that she can read.

Listening to a child read a sentence or two should provide the teacher with clues to her word attack ability. A hypothesis that a particular skill is lacking can be tested by having the child read words or sentences containing words that call for her to make the letter-sound relationships that fit the hypothesis. If this simple, informal test discloses a problem, the teacher selects or develops appropriate materials and works simultaneously with all students who can profit from the instruction decided upon.

What we know about children and how they learn dictates that we accept the premise that all children in a given classroom do not need identical amounts of phonics instruction. Most phonics instruction materials do not make provision for student differences. Differentiation of instruction in this area is primarily the task of the teacher, just as it is in all areas of the curriculum.

Is It Possible to Teach Children to Overrely on Phonic Analysis?

Children can be taught to overrely on phonics, or on sight words, or on guessing from context. Overreliance on any one skill is bad for learners because they inevitably fail to utilize all the available cues. Thus, flexibility and efficiency are diminished.

The beginning reader should be receiving instruction that helps her crack the code, but she is handicapped if she relies too heavily on phonic analysis. If a child can and does sound out every word in a story, she is not becoming an efficient reader. She is analyzing some words long after she should have mastered them as sight words; that is, she may be sounding words the 10th, 20th, or 50th time she meets them. Since the objective of reading instruction is not to produce this kind of reader, every effort should be made to see that the child does not generalize that sounding out words is reading.

Should Children Still Be Taught
Sight Words in Beginning Reading?

Starting from the premise that a child must learn to associate printed letter symbols with speech sounds does not negate the fact that one must also learn to recognize whole words. Whenever a child is making normal progress in learning to read, he is increasing his sight vocabulary or stock of words that he recognizes instantly. At the end of first grade he will have a larger sight vocabulary than at the end of 5 months of instruction and practice. At the conclusion of second grade, his sight vocabulary will be much larger than it was at the beginning of that school year. The skill that best illustrates the developmental nature of reading is acquisition of a sight vocabulary. When a reader meets words he recognizes, he does not apply phonic analysis. He knows what spoken word the printed form represents; therefore, there is nothing to solve through letter-sound analysis.

Also, the irregular spellings of many English words limit the effectiveness of phonic analysis and dictate that these words be learned as sight words (*know, once, head, give, great, have, many, love, does, one, done, here, of, said, too, use, very, gone, should, who, some, put, move, none, son, two*). In addition, a number of words appear so frequently in English speech and writing that it would be wasteful to sound out those words each time they are met. For example, after only a few weeks of reading instruction centering on normal English usage, a child will have met each of the following words often: *can, made, say, stop, keep, like, not, man, sun, make, run, at,* and *bring.*

PRINCIPLES TO APPLY IN TEACHING PHONICS

The systematic study of any teaching-learning situation may be expected to yield a set of psychologically sound principles that relate to and govern teaching procedures. In teaching, one would follow sound principles so as to enhance learning. Principles do not spell out precise practices to follow, but rather they provide a set of guidelines by which to measure classroom instructional practices. The following principles for teaching phonic analysis are offered for teachers' consideration.

- *For any child to profit from systematic phonics instruction, he must be able to differentiate among different speech sounds in words and visually discriminate among printed letters.* The absence of either of these prerequisites would preclude learning letter-sound relationships. For example, a child who can differentiate between the sounds of *bee* and *dee* but cannot visually discriminate between the printed symbols *b* and *d* cannot apply phonics in a reading situation involving words that contain these symbols.
- *Practices followed in beginning reading do tend to inculcate a mind set in the learner.* Instruction should not lead the child to think of reading as consisting of either learning sight words or sounding letters or relying on context clues. Such instruction is likely to result in overreliance on one or another of these essential skills.
- *Instructional practices should ensure that beginning readers learn all essential word identification skills.* Overreliance on any one skill can impair reading efficiency.
- *All necessary phonic skills (letter-sound relationships) the child needs to become an independent reader should be taught.*
- *All elementary teachers should be familiar with the entire phonics program.* All teachers of reading, regardless of grade level, will probably find it necessary to teach, review, or reteach certain phonic skills to some children in their classrooms. Thus, familiarity with all steps in phonics instruction is essential.
- *Diagnosis is essential for discovering each child's present needs, and diagnosis is the basis for differentiation of instruction.*
- *The spelling patterns in English writing limit the usefulness of certain rules or generalizations.* Little value may reside in teaching a generalization that applies to only a few words or that has numerous exceptions.

SUMMARY

Beginning readers must master letter-sound relationships and apply this knowledge as they learn to read. To become facile readers, children must use *all* word identification skills. However, overreliance on any one skill, such as learning sight words, using context clues, or applying phonic analysis, can interfere with growth in reading ability. The optimum amount of phonics for every child is the minimum that child needs to become an independent reader.

PREREQUISITES FOR PHONICS INSTRUCTION

VISUAL DISCRIMINATION

Children will have had innumerable experiences in making visual discriminations before they enter school and are called upon to make the much finer discriminations required in reading. The school will then provide many readiness activities that foster visual discrimination. Some of these may be only vaguely related to learning to read—matching objects and geometric forms, noting missing parts of pictures, and the like.

Other activities will relate more closely to the tasks required in reading. Studies have established that the ability to name the letters of the alphabet is one of the best predictors of a child's success in beginning reading. However, naming letters is a memory-association skill and is really not the crucial issue. The importance of being able to name letters is that it establishes that the child can discriminate visually among the various letter forms. Children have an almost uncanny ability to learn names or labels. Thus, teaching letter names is not the primary goal, but the ability to name letters is the criterion for establishing visual discrimination of graphic forms.

● MATCHING AND NAMING LETTER FORMS

1. Match Letters

Duplicate exercises similar to the following illustration. The children circle or trace each letter on the line that is exactly like the stimulus on the left.

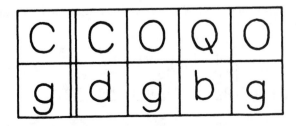

2. Flash Card Drill

a. Prepare large flash cards for each letter of the alphabet. Hold up a card and select a volunteer to name the letter or have the group name the letter in unison.

b. Prepare smaller letter-cards for each participant with the same letter form on the front and back of the card.

Hand out identical card groups of three or four to all participants, who spread the cards on their desks. Give directions: "Hold up the letter *m*," etc. Observe children who are having difficulty and provide added practice for these students.

3. Build a Pile

a. This is a game for two or more children. Use a pack of letter cards, each of which has a letter form on one side only.

b. The cards are placed face down and the first player draws a card. He shows the card, and if he names the letter he places it face down in his pile.

c. When a player fails to name the letter, the next player may try to name it and place it in her pile. Then she draws a card.

d. At the end of the game, the player with the most cards wins.

4. Two-letter Sequence

Duplicate a series of two-letter words. Instruct children to circle each word that is exactly like the stimulus at the left.

it		at	in	up	it
on		of	on	no	on
is		as	us	is	so

5. Three-letter Sequence

This is for added difficulty; use the same instructions as for Two-letter Sequence using three-letter words.

sat		hat	sat	say	sad
can		cat	pan	can	cap
dug		dug	bug	dog	dug

● MATCHING CAPITAL AND LOWERCASE LETTERS

1. The children draw a line from the capital letter at the left of the box to the matching lowercase letter at the right of the box.

A------ a	b a e	B	b c p	E	a m e
G	g n r	H	d g h	R	d r f

2. Duplicate a page of boxes, each containing two letter forms. The children circle each pair of letters that contains both a capital and lowercase form of the same letter.

Hh	Ee	Fg	Bb
Ba	Gg	Dd	Aa

3. Prepare a series of cards similar to those used for the Flash Card Drill. (Each participant has lowercase letter cards for each letter in the exercise.) Place one capital letter form on the chalk tray. Call on a volunteer to place the matching lowercase letter below the capital form shown. Continue through the cards.

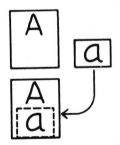

4. a. Duplicate Tic-Tac-Toe pages of squares composed of three-by-three smaller squares.
b. Each set should have a capital letter in the center square and a variety of lowercase letters in all other squares. These should be arranged so that one line contains the capital and two lowercase forms of the same letter.
c. Have the children draw a line through the three squares that contain the same letter form.

● TRACING LETTER FORMS

1. Print a large letter form on the chalkboard. Trace the form and say the letter name while children trace the form in the air and repeat the letter name.

2. Prepare duplicated pages showing a heavy-line letter form on the left and dotted letter outlines on the balance of the line. Children trace over the dots to form the letters.

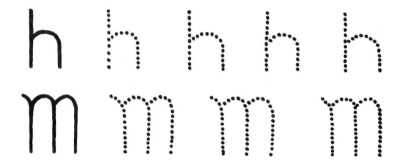

3. Duplicate a page of letter stimuli as shown. The children trace each letter outline that will result in the same letter as the stimulus at the left.

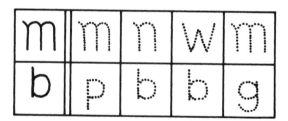

4. Prepare duplicated pages of letters as shown. After tracing the first letter outlined, the children print the letter in each of the remaining boxes on the line.

5. Prepare a page of letter symbols, each of which is followed by a partially completed letter. The children are to add the part that is missing in order to complete the letter shown at the left.

 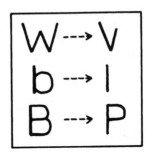 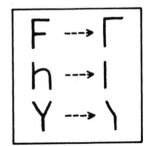

● **DISCRIMINATION OF WORD FORMS**

In this task, children do not have to be able to name the words; they simply underline every word in the box that is the same as the stimulus word at the left. Exercises progress from gross differences to minimum differences.

lake	small	the	lake	name
word	take	word	each	word

ball	ball	fill	bat	ball
come	call	come	come	love

cat	can	cat	rat	cat
hand	band	sand	hand	hand

AUDITORY DISCRIMINATION

Learning to read involves both the ability to make finer and finer visual discriminations among printed word symbols and the ability to associate oral speech sounds with printed letters and letter combinations. These are often referred to as *mechanical skills*, whose value is sometimes downgraded in comparison with the so-called higher-level comprehension skills. Jt is a mistake to argue the relative virtues of decoding and comprehension in beginning reading, since both are absolutely essential ingredients in the process of learning to read.

Phonics instruction is related to previous learnings. Prior to reading, children have had many auditory experiences with language that bear directly on learning to read. Upon entering school, children

Can differentiate among thousands of words spoken by other individuals

Can use thousands of words in their own speech

Have developed concepts for thousands of words

Successfully teaching all subsequent steps in phonic analysis is based on the child's ability to discriminate among speech sounds in words. The ability to make or use all English speech sounds in words does not assure the ability to discriminate among individual phonemes in words. Children learn spoken words as global units and can easily distinguish among words with minimal phoneme differences. Phonics instruction aims at instant association of a particular sound with a given letter or letters. Thus, if a child cannot distinguish the minute auditory differences being taught in a particular phonics lesson, she cannot profit from that instruction.

Occasionally, children are fairly successful in learning consonant sounds but have trouble mastering certain vowel sounds. An example of such a case is a high school student who could not differentiate between spoken words containing the short sound of *e* or *i.* Pairs of words, which differed only in the vowel in medial position, were numbered for identification purposes. The tutor would say one of the words and ask the boy to give the number of the word pronounced. His responses demonstrated conclusively that he could not aurally distinguish between words such as those in the following pairs:

A. (1) bet (2) bit		**D.** (1) pen (2) pin
B. (1) Ben (2) bin		**E.** (1) bed (2) bid
C. (1) mitt (2) met		**F.** (1) then (2) thin

Many hours of practice were required for the boy to overcome this deficiency. A tape recorder was used as the tutor and the boy read words from identical lists. The tutor would pronounce a word, then the boy would say the same word using the tutor's pronunciation as a model. The student listened to the recordings many times before he was able to differentiate between these vowel sounds.

Dialects

A related question is how dialects impinge on phonics instruction, and on learning to read. There is little research that purports to provide definitive data about how hearing and speaking nonstandard dialects affect learning to read Standard, or textbook, English. However, children in Georgia, Vermont, and southern Illinois do learn to read using the same text materials printed in Standard English. This is not surprising, because the term *dialect* means "a pattern of pronunciation, grammar, and vocabulary that can be understood by practitioners of the various dialects of a given language."

In recent years Black English has been studied extensively because it creates a number of phonological differences from words in Standard English. Examples include initial *th* sounded as *d* (dat, dem) and dropping the final consonant sounds *t, d,* and *r.* This has resulted in the creation of a number of homonyms not present in Standard English: told = toll; floor = flo(w); mind = min(e); past = pas(s); hold = hol(e)/whole. It must be remembered, however, that in reading, words such as these are confronted not in isolation but in context. Thus, reading for meaning tends to minimize any detrimental effects that might be attributed to phonological differences found in various dialects.

Initial Sounds in Words

The procedures a teacher might use to help children develop skill in auditory discrimination are practically unlimited. The following are illustrative.

1. Children listen while the teacher pronounces a series of words, all of which begin with the same consonant sound: b*elt*, b*all*, b*ird*, b*e*, and b*one*. Children then volunteer other words that begin with the same sound: b*aby*, b*ug*, b*at*, b*oom*, and b*ang*.

2. Pairs of pictures are grouped by initial sound. Collect a number of pictures from workbooks, catalogues, or magazines. Paste each picture on a separate piece of cardboard to make handling easier. Select several pairs of pictures whose naming words begin with the same sound. The children then group these according to initial sound (ball-boat; house-horse; fence-feather; pig-pumpkin; log-ladder).

As the children progress, the difficulty level of the exercise can be increased by including three or more pictures whose names begin with the same sound. Of course, the objects in the pictures should be known by the children.

3. Obtain pictures that contain many objects (advertisements, etc.).

Teacher: "Do you see an object that begins with the sound we hear at the beginning of the names *Billy* and *Betty*?" (ball, basket)

"Do you see a picture of something that begins with the sound we hear at the beginning of the words *hand* and *help*?" (hat, horse)

Continue to use stimulus words whose initial sound matches that of naming words for objects pictured.

4. Prepare a series of picture strips, each containing a stimulus picture at the left and three or four other pictures. The children name a picture only if its name begins with the same sound as the picture at the left. Always identify picture names before children work independently, to avoid the confusion of their calling a pail a bucket or a fox a dog, and so on.

● WORKING WITH RHYMES

The purpose of the following activities is to provide practice in discriminating speech sounds in words, specifically rhyming elements. In addition, the exercises focus on developing other skills such as (a) listening (limiting responses to one category: e.g., numbers, colors, or animals), (b) following directions, and (c) noting stress and intonation patterns.

1. Matching Rhyming Picture Names

Place on the bulletin board or chalk tray a number of mixed-together pairs of pictures whose naming words rhyme. Children volunteer to remove two pictures whose naming words rhyme. The child then names the pictures:

"This is a dog.
This is a log.
Dog and log rhyme."

2. Thinking of Rhyming Words

Explain that you are going to read some sentences. Children are to listen carefully so they can supply words that rhyme with the last word in each sentence. The last word in the sentence should be stressed; in some classroom situations it may even be advisable to repeat it once.

1. Be sure to wear a hat on your *head*. (red, bed, Ted, said)
2. We will take a trip to the *lake*.
3. John, you may pet the *cat*.
4. They all said hello to the *man*.
5. Have you ever seen a *moose?*
6. We watched the bird build its *nest*.
7. Let's all count to *ten*.
8. Mary walked in the rain and got *wet*.
9. Sunday, we went to the *beach*.

Variation: Prepare sentences in which the final word is omitted. In reading the sentence, emphasize one word. A child completes the sentence by giving a word that rhymes with the word that is emphasized. This procedure also teaches the concept of stress as part of intonation patterns.

1. A *frog* sat on a _____. (log)

2. Mary will *bake* a chocolate _____. (cake)

3. Please do not bounce the *ball* in the _____. (hall)

4. On his finger the *king* wore a _____. (ring)

5. Kate will *wait* by the _____ (gate)

6. Keith swept the *room* with a nice new _____. (broom)

3. Number Rhymes

Explain that you will pronounce and emphasize two words that rhyme with a number word. The children are to supply the rhyming number word to finish each sentence.

1. *Blue* and *shoe* rhyme with _____. (two)

2. *Gate* and *hate* rhyme with _____. (eight)

3. *Fix* and *mix* rhyme with _____. (six)

4. *Drive* and *hive* rhyme with _____. (five)

5. *Gun* and *run* rhyme with _____. (one)

6. *Tree* and *see* rhyme with _____. (three)

7. *When* and *then* rhyme with _____. (ten)

8. *Pine* and *line* rhyme with _____. (nine)

9. *Door* and *more* rhyme with _____. (four)

10. *Eleven* and *heaven* rhyme with _____. (seven)

To provide practice in speaking in sentences, have one volunteer say the entire sentence after each rhyme: "*Gate* and *late* rhyme with *eight.*"

Variation: This activity is similar to the preceding one except that the last word you speak is the clue to the rhyming word.

Teacher: "Give me a number that rhymes with _____."

1. *fun* (one)　　　　　　**6.** *hen* (ten)

2. *fix* (six)　　　　　　**7.** *late* (eight)

3. *fine* (nine)　　　　　**8.** *do* (two)

4. *floor* (four)　　　　　**9.** *alive* (five)

5. *bee* (three)　　　　　**10.** *heaven* (seven)

4. Color Names to Complete a Rhyme

Teacher: "Name the color that rhymes with _____."

1. *head* and *bed* (red)

2. *clean* and *queen* (green)

3. *tray* and *play* (gray)
4. *do* and *you* (blue)
5. *track* and *back* (black)
6. *town* and *gown* (brown)
7. *man* and *ran* (tan)
8. *sight* and *kite* (white)
9. *think* and *sink* (pink)
10. *fellow* and *Jell-O* (yellow)

5. Animal Names to Complete a Rhyme

Teacher: "Name an animal that rhymes with _____."

1. *hat* (rat, cat)   **6.** *near* (deer)
2. *log* (dog, frog)   **7.** *jeep* (sheep)
3. *house* (mouse)   **8.** *cantaloupe* (antelope)
4. *boat* (goat)   **9.** *big* (pig)
5. *mitten* (kitten)   **10.** *box* (fox)

6. Rhyming Words and Following Directions

Each participant should have two 3″ × 5″ cards with the word *yes* printed on both sides of one card, and *no* printed on both sides of the other. Read statements similar to those below. If the two emphasized words rhyme, children hold up the *yes* card; if the words do not rhyme, they hold up the *no* card.

1. I say *fox* and *box.* (yes)
2. I say *coat* and *road.* (no)
3. I say *found* and *ground.* (yes)
4. I say *man* and *men.* (no)
5. I say *car* and *cart.* (no)
6. I say *feet* and *meet.* (yes)
7. I say *book* and *look.* (yes)
8. I say *glass* and *dress.* (no)
9. I say *bug* and *rug.* (yes)
10. I say *chair* and *church.* (no)

7. Forming Rhymes with Letter Names

Teacher: "Name a letter (or letters) that rhymes with _____." or "What letter(s) rhymes with _____?"

1. *say* and *day* (a, k, j)
2. *me* and *tree* (b, c, d, e, g, v, t, z, p)
3. *sell* and *bell* (l)
4. *hen* and *ten* (n)
5. *high* and *sky* (i, y)
6. *far* and *car* (r)
7. *true* and *blue* (u, q)
8. *them* and *gem* (m)
9. *no* and *grow* (o)
10. *dress* and *less* (s)

8. Picture Rhymes

Duplicate a series of boxes, each containing either three or four pictures. Select pictures so that two naming words rhyme. Children are to draw a line connecting these two pictures.

Teacher: "Name the pictures. Two will rhyme. Connect these pictures every time."

Final Sounds in Words

Besides practice in initial sounds and rhyming elements, children need auditory practice in matching and differentiating the final sound in words (nonrhyming elements). It is easier for children to note that *cat* and *rat* end with the same sounds than it is to note that *cat* and *tent* end with the same sound.

Drills and practice in final sounds can be provided by adapting procedures and approaches cited earlier, as well as by using the following exercises.

1. Pairs of Words

Pronounce pairs of words, some of which end with the same sound. If the two words end with the same sound, the children respond "same"; if the final sounds are different, they say "different."

  1. *net* and *but* (same)
  2. *fan* and *fat* (different)
  3. *fog* and *pig* (same)
  4. *hen* and *man* (same)
  5. *six* and *tax* (same)
  6. *bus* and *gas* (same)
  7. *hat* and *hid* (different)
  8. *leg* and *let* (different)
  9. *rub* and *rug* (different)
  10. *lip* and *tap* (same)
  11. *hop* and *hot* (different)
  12. *log* and *bug* (same)

Start with C-V-C words and gradually include longer words.

2. Using Pictures

Prepare a series of picture strips or duplicate a page consisting of lines containing four or five pictures. Students underline each picture whose name ends with the same sound as the stimulus picture at the left.

SUMMARY

The exercises in this chapter dealt with teaching visual discrimination of letters and words and with noting speech sounds in words. These two skills are prerequisites for phonics instruction, which has been defined as "teaching letter-sound relationships." Thus far, children have not been asked to associate a given letter form with a specific speech sound. The next two chapters focus on teaching this skill.

5

CONSONANT LETTER-SOUND RELATIONSHIPS

We have so far dealt with skills that are prerequisites for learning letter-sound relationships. The two major skills are the ability to discriminate among letter forms and the ability to differentiate auditorily among speech sounds as heard in words. This chapter will focus on teaching that combines these skills and leads children to associate a particular sound with a specific letter or combination of letters.

A WORD ABOUT SEQUENCE

The phonics program consists of teaching many specific skills. In any systematic program, this myriad of skills would have to be arranged into some teaching sequence. There are some options in regard to sequence that undoubtedly are of little educational consequence (such as whether to teach the sound of *t* before *b*, or *m* before *n*). On the other hand, the question of whether to teach consonant or vowel letter-sounds first is worthy of consideration.

Rationale for Teaching Consonant Sounds First

The majority of words children meet in beginning reading are words that begin with consonants. For instance, 175 (or approximately 80%) of the 220 words on the Dolch Basic Sight Word Test begin with consonants. The Dale List of 769 Easy Words contains an even higher proportion (87%) of words beginning with consonants.

It is good learning theory to have children start phonic analysis with the beginnings of words, working their way through the words from left to right. This reinforces the practice of reading from left to right and focuses children's attention on the first part of the word. This is essential for facile reading and an absolute prerequisite if children are to solve the word by sounding.

Consonants tend to be much more consistent than vowels in the sounds they represent. For instance, a number of consonants (*j, k, l, m, n, p, b, h, r, v, w*) represent only one sound. Certain other consonants that have two sounds present no problem in beginning reading instruction because one of the two basic sounds can be left un-til the child has had considerable practice in reading.

If a child uses skills in combination, sounding the initial consonant letter and us-ing context-meaning clues will frequently be all the analysis that is needed. Assume each blank line in the following examples represents an unknown word:

1. _____ (This could represent any of 600,000 words in English.)

2. f_____ (Here, more than 98% of all words are eliminated. The unknown word must begin with the sound associated with the letter *f.*)

It is probable that the reader will arrive at the unknown word(s) in the following sen-tences despite the very limited context that is provided:

3. "You will have to pay the f_____ now," said the judge.

4. Without a doubt, pumpkin is my f_____ pie.

5. He took the stolen jewels to the f_____.

6. During J_____ it is much colder than it is in J_____ and J_____.

The sequence of teachings suggested in this chapter is:

1. Initial consonant letter-sounds
2. Initial consonant blends or clusters (*bl, st,* etc.)
3. Initial consonant digraphs (*ch, wh, sh, th,* etc.)
4. Final consonants, blends, and digraphs
5. Consonant irregularities

Listing this sequence does not imply that all the possible steps under 1 must be com-pleted before introducing any of the teachings in 2, 3, 4, or 5. The procedures that follow illustrate some of the many approaches that can be used in teaching letter-sound relationships.

INITIAL CONSONANT LETTER-SOUNDS

One widely used technique for teaching initial letter-sounds is the use of children's names.

1. Write the names of several children in the class (or other common first names) that begin with the same letter (Bill, Beth, Ben, Brad) on the chalkboard.

2. Pronounce each name; then have the class pronounce each name.

3. Call attention to the fact that each name begins with the same letter, and that this letter (*B*) represents the same sound in each word.

4. Use other series of names for other letter-sounds.

Jason	Denise	Mary	Steven
Josh	Daniel	Matthew	Suzy
Jill	Devon	Mike	Simon
Jamie	David	Maggie	Sarah

Other techniques for teaching initial letter-sounds follow.

1. Chalkboard Drill

For purposes of illustration, we will give the steps for teaching the sound of the consonant *m* in detail. All other consonant sounds can be taught in the same manner.

a. Print the letter *m* (capital and lowercase) on the chalkboard. Indicate that for the next few minutes the group will study the sound of the letter *m* as it is heard in words. Write on the board a column of previously studied words, all of which begin with the letter *m*.

b. Any words the children have met (as sight words) in experience charts or other materials may be used—words such as *me, must, moon,* and *mind.* Also, familiar names and names of children in the class that call for capital letters may be used.

<u>M</u>	<u>m</u>
Mary	my
Mike	most
	man
	much
	milk

c. Ask the children to look at the words carefully and name the letter that begins each word. Indicate that a big *M* or capital letter is used in names.

d. As you pronounce the words, ask the children to listen to the sound heard at the beginning of each word. The initial sound should be emphasized but not distorted.

e. The children are then invited to read the words in unison, listening carefully to the sound of *m* as they say the words.

f. Ask children to supply other words that begin with the sound of *m*.

2. Match a Pair

This game is an adaptation of Concentration; it involves the use of pictures and two or more children as participants (individual or team play).

Select pairs of pictures so that two picture-naming words begin with the same letter-sound: h*orse*—h*and;* be*ll*—*boat;* t*able*—*tub;* f*ish*—*fox;* and de*sk*—d*uck.* Shuffle the cards and lay them face down on the table.

The first player turns up two cards, hoping to match a pair of initial letter-sounds. If the player is successful, she picks up both cards. If she does not match initial letter-sounds, both cards are again turned face down. Other players continue taking turns. Each player attempts to note and remember the location of pictures that have been turned up but not matched.

The winner is the player or team with the most pictures at the end of the game.

3. Building a Picture Dictionary

Use a supply of pictures from workbooks, magazines, and catalogues. Work with one letter at a time, *B—b,* for example.

After teaching the initial sound of *B—b* in words, have the children gather pictures whose naming words begin with that letter-sound. Children may work individually or in small groups.

Prepare a page (or several pages) for each letter-sound. Print a capital and lowercase letter at the top of the page and fill the page with pictures whose naming words begin with that letter-sound.

B - b

boot	bird	bed
bus	basket	book
barn	boat	boy

4. Print and Sound

Compile columns of easy words that begin with the letter-sounds to be taught or reviewed. Delete the initial letter of each word, and provide space for students to write the letter.

As they print the initial letter, the children pronounce the word they have formed. (Material may be presented on the chalkboard, with transparencies, or as duplicated exercises.) Here are several examples:

a. *Teacher:* "In each blank space, add the letter above the column of words. Pronounce each word."

t	s	c	l
__ag	__ad	__ap	__og
__ub	__ix	__ot	__ap
__en	__un	__up	__ed
__op	__it	__an	__eg
__ip	__ob	__ub	__et

b. *Teacher:* "In each blank space, write one of the letters *h, w,* or *g.* Be sure the letter you choose makes a word. Pronounce the word."

__im	__ot	__ip	__ub
__et	__un	__ad	__id
__um	__at	__ig	__ug
__eb	__en	__ap	__em

c. *Teacher:* "In each blank space, add any letter that will make a word."

__ug	__og	__eg	__at
__ox	__un	__it	__op
__ad	__ig	__ub	__in
__en	__an	__ot	__us

Mental Substitution

Day by day, in the early stages of reading instruction, the child is learning both sight words and the sounds of initial consonants. Knowledge thus gained can be applied in arriving at the pronunciation of other words not known as sight words. Assume the child knows the words *king* and *ring* and meets the unknown word *sing.* He should be able to combine the *s* sound, which he knows in words like *sat, some,* and *say,* with the sound of *ing* found in *king* and *ring.* This involves a process of "thinking the sounds." To illustrate, let us assume the following:

1. A child has learned the italicized words in Table 5–1.
2. He has learned the sounds of the initial consonants as heard in the italicized words.
3. He has not met or learned any of the other 34 words in Table 5–1.
4. By using his knowledge, plus some guidance from the teacher, he should be able to sound out all the words in Table 5–1.

By using the process of thinking the sound of any known consonant and blending this sound with the phonogram that concludes a known sight word, the child should be able to pronounce the new word.

Other techniques for teaching mental substitution follow.

TABLE 5–1 Identifying Words Using Mental Substitution

bat	can	fit	had	map	pet	run	say
cat	ban	bit	bad	cap	bet	bun	bay
fat	fan	hit	fad	rap	met	fun	hay
hat	man	pit	mad	sap	set	sun	may
mat	pan	sit	pad				pay
pat	ran		sad				ray
rat							

1. Place a known word on the board. Have the children observe closely as you erase the initial *b* and substitute a different known consonant.

bat __at cat

Follow the same procedure, substituting other consonants to make easy words, such as *fat, hat, mat,* and *rat.*

For convenience in building mental substitution exercises, Table 5–2 provides a series of word families. In each, the words end in a common phonogram (*et, ick, ack, ay, ot, an, ill, im, ug, ad,* etc.). Not all the words in the table need to be used in beginning reading, and those beginning with blends should not be used in substitution exercises until the sounds of the blends have been taught.

2. *Teacher:* "Change the first letter and make a naming word for 'something living.' "

Example:
dish __ish fish

log	__og	hat	__at	half	__alf
coat	__oat	purse	__urse	nice	__ice
box	__ox	mitten	__itten	grow	__row
house	__ouse	rug	__ug	pull	__ull

3. *Teacher:* "On the line following each word, write a new word by changing the first letter to the next letter in the alphabet. Then pronounce the new word and use it in a sentence."

bake	_____	cot	_____	fun	_____
ball	_____	cry	_____	fame	_____
book	_____	candy	_____	fate	_____
but	_____	crop	_____	fold	_____
gold	_____	lad	_____	met	_____
got	_____	lake	_____	moon	_____
gate	_____	let	_____	mine	_____
gum	_____	line	_____	meat	_____
		lap	_____	mice	_____

TABLE 5–2 Words for Teaching Substitution of Initial Consonant Sounds
(Words with initial consonant blends are in parentheses.)

back	bake	day	cap	bug	bank	cot	Dick
Jack	cake	hay	gap	dug	rank	dot	kick
lack	fake	lay	lap	hug	sank	got	lick
pack	lake	may	map	jug	tank	hot	nick
rack	make	pay	nap	mug	(blank)	lot	pick
sack	rake	ray	rap	rug	(crank)	not	sick
tack	sake	say	tap	tug	(drank)	pot	(brick)
(black)	take	way	(clap)	(drug)	(flank)	(blot)	(click)
(crack)	wake	(clay)	(flap)	(plug)	(frank)	(plot)	(slick)
(slack)	(brake)	(play)	(slap)	(slug)	(plank)	(shot)	(stick)
(stack)	(flake)	(stray)	(snap)	(smug)	(prank)	(spot)	(thick)
(track)	(snake)	(tray)	(trap)	(snug)	(spank)	(trot)	(trick)
bag	bail	gain	bat	bump	can	came	Bill
gag	fail	lain	cat	dump	Dan	dame	fill
lag	hail	main	fat	hump	fan	fame	hill
nag	mail	pain	hat	jump	man	game	kill
rag	nail	rain	mat	lump	pan	lame	mill
sag	pail	vain	pat	pump	ran	name	pill
tag	rail	(brain)	rat	(plump)	tan	same	will
wag	sail	(drain)	sat	(slump)	van	tame	(drill)
(brag)	tail	(grain)	(brat)	(stump)	(bran)	(blame)	(skill)
(drag)	(frail)	(plain)	(flat)	(trump)	(clan)	(flame)	(spill)
(flag)	(trail)	(train)	(scat)		(plan)	(frame)	(still)
(snag)	(snail)						
best	bet	bunk	bell	bit	dim	dear	bad
lest	get	dunk	fell	fit	him	fear	dad
nest	jet	hunk	sell	hit	Jim	hear	fad
pest	let	junk	tell	pit	rim	near	had
rest	met	sunk	well	sit	Tim	rear	lad
test	net	(drunk)	yell	wit	(brim)	tear	mad
vest	pet	(flunk)	(smell)	(flit)	(grim)	year	pad
zest	set	(skunk)	(spell)	(grit)	(slim)	(clear)	sad
(blest)	wet	(spunk)	(swell)	(slit)	(swim)	(smear)	(glad)
(crest)	(fret)	(trunk)		(split)	(trim)	(spear)	

Difficulty level can be increased by mixing the words instead of presenting a series of four words.

boat _____   map _____   sail _____

cash _____   run _____   rat _____

fang _____   sight _____   bold _____

ray	_____	bat	_____	sack	_____
kit	_____	kick	_____	ring	_____
lay	_____	vest	_____	kid	_____

Context Plus Minimal Phonic Cue

The following exercise illustrates that, in many situations, the context plus the phonic cue provided by the initial letter of an unknown word will provide enough clues to solve the unknown word. The blank space in each sentence under A could be replaced with several different words. The same blank space in the corresponding sentence under B provides the initial consonant letter of the word. Have children note that when they heed this phonic cue, they can eliminate many of the previously acceptable choices.

Directions: Read the sentences under A. Have children provide a number of words that could fit in each blank. Then read the sentences under B and have the children note their general agreement on choices.

A

1. The _____ would not start.

2. "She is my _____," said Billy.

3. Billy asked, "How much _____ do we have?"

4. Which _____ of the year is your favorite?

5. What word _____ in the blank space?

B

1. The c_____ would not start.

2. "She is my s_____," said Billy.

3. Billy asked, "How much m_____ do we have?"

4. Which t_____ of the year is your favorite?

5. What word f_____ in the blank space?

Oral Exercise

Directions: Have a volunteer read one of the following incomplete sentences, adding any word that will logically conclude the sentence. Other students then volunteer other words that fit. Stress that no word can fit unless it begins with the sound represented by the letter shown.

Written Exercise

Directions: Children write one (or more) words that begin with the letter shown.

1. Can you see the p_____?

2. Is this your b_____?

3. This is a t_____.

4. Here is the d_____.

5. The girls felt very s_____.

CONTEXT CLUES AND PHONIC SKILLS: WORKING TOGETHER

Under less than optimal teaching practices, phonics instruction can be so far removed from reading that it inhibits learning to read. All phonics instruction, however, need not focus exclusively on letter-sound relationships. Reading instruction can be made more effective if the learning task involves both reading (context) and a phonics task whose completion depends on the reading task.

In this chapter, as well as in following chapters, phonics instruction is imbedded in a "Fun with Language" approach. The learner is asked to read in order to discover what phonics task he is being asked to perform. The difficulty levels of these exercises range from one-word clues to phrases and sentences. These materials can be adapted to almost any phonic teaching: initial, medial, and final consonants; blends, digraphs, and vowel patterns. In all of these exercises, the teacher reads the directions and any sample items with the student.

● USING CONTEXT

Teacher: "Read the clue. What do they do? Write the correct word in the space."

Clue			Clue		
dogs	_____	(bark, dark)	cows	_____	(moo, boo)
birds	_____	(sly, fly)	bells	_____	(wing, ring)
boats	_____	(hail, sail)	fires	_____	(turn, burn)
horses	_____	(run, fun)	kings	_____	(mule, rule)
towels	_____	(cry, dry)	frogs	_____	(hop, mop)

Teacher: "Read the clue. Complete the word that fits the clue. Use one of the letters *c* or *t* to make a word that fits the clue."

Example:

	pretty	__ute	use c to spell *cute*
	story	__ale	use t to spell *tale*

Clue			Clue		
1. money	__ash		**6.** speaking	__alk	
2. bath	__ub		**7.** knives	__ut	
3. brush	__eeth		**8.** Christmas	__ard	
4. bird	__age		**9.** gentle	__ame	
5. spins	__op		**10.** penny	__ent	

Teacher: "Write one of the letters *p* or *n* in each blank space to make a word that fits the clue."

	Clue			*Clue*	
1.	fruit	___ear	**6.**	loud	___oise
2.	bird	___est	**7.**	medicine	___ill
3.	fence	___ost	**8.**	pecan kernel	___ut
4.	two	___air	**9.**	sharp	___eedle
5.	close	___ear	**10.**	writes	___en

Teacher: "Read the clue. Add the first letter to make a word that fits the clue."

Example:

you can read it ___ook (b)

	Clue			*Clue*	
1.	not small	___ig	**6.**	season before winter	___all
2.	lives on a farm	___ig	**7.**	not short	___all
3.	false hair	___ig	**8.**	round and bounces	___all
4.	a dance step	___ig	**9.**	from floor to ceiling	___all
5.	make a hole in the ground	___ig	**10.**	shopping center	___all

Teacher: "Write the letter that spells the word that fits the clue. Use *p, b,* or *d.*"

	Clue			*Clue*	
1.	we read it	___ook	**6.**	goes around waist	___elt
2.	please open the	___oor	**7.**	we sleep on it	___ed
3.	lives on a farm	___ig	**8.**	worth 10 cents	___ime
4.	goes on the water	___oat	**9.**	place where we play	___ark
5.	a dog is a	___et	**10.**	at night it is	___ark

Teacher: "Change the first letter in each underlined word so that the new word names something living."

Examples:

I can change big to ___ig. (*pig*)

I can change see to ___ee. (*bee*)

I can change: hat to ___at

dish to ___ish

pen to ___en

toy to ___oy

If a child or group has difficulty with a particular consonant letter sound, develop exercises that focus on this letter. (The exercise that follows illustrates *c* and *f*.)

Teacher: "Read the clue. Write the letter that spells the word that fits the clue."

Set 1		Set 2	
Clue		*Clue*	
1. wear on head	__ap	**1.** not slow	__ast
2. catches mice	__at	**2.** lives in water	__ish
3. not hot	__old	**3.** more than four	__ive
4. grows on farm	__orn	**4.** after summer	__all
5. baby cow	__alf	**5.** less than five	__our
6. ice cream	__one	**6.** good to eat	__ood
7. a baby bear	__ub	**7.** a tree	__ir

● **FUN WITH LANGUAGE**

1. Fun with D, F, S, and G Words

Teacher: "Read the clues. Be careful; they're tricky. Complete the word that fits the clue. Use one of the consonant letters *d, f, s,* or *g* to spell the word that fits the clue."

Example:

Clue		
not much money	__ime	*d* is the only letter that fits the clue; a dime is not much money.
front of head	__ace	Choose *f;* it makes sense.
four legs and butts	__oat	*g* makes goat, which has four legs. Have you ever heard of a goat butting someone?

Clue		*Clue*	
1. not back, not front	__ide	**6.** Don't _____ the bears.	__eed
2. 1492 . . . . 1776 1976	__ates	**7.** always number one	__irst
3. hole-in-one	__olf	**8.** not here now	__one
4. damp minus *p*	__am	**9.** what I owe you	__ebt
5. goes in shoes	__eet	**10.** like the others	__ame

2. The 3-C Sentences!

In the sentences below:

    A. Candy is a girl's name. (Candy starts with a capital letter!)
    B. She has a candy cane.
    C. The three c's get all mixed up, but when you read for meaning it's easy.

Teacher: "Fill in each blank space with one of these words: *Candy, candy,* or *cane.*"

Problem: _____ has a _____ _____.

Solved: Candy has a candy cane.

    1. Does _____ have a _____ _____?

2. Yes, the _____ _____ belongs to _____.

3. Will _____ eat her _____ _____?

4. _____ may eat the _____ _____.

5. Then _____ will not have a _____ _____.

6. This ends the story of _____ and her _____ _____.

3. B(ware)—B(ready)—B(sharp)

Teacher: "Every blank space in the following sentences can be filled with the following B words: *book, boy,* or *bus.* As you read each sentence write the correct word in each blank space."

1. The _____ has a _____.

2. The _____ took the _____ on a _____.

3. The _____ left the _____ on the _____.

4. The _____ driver found the _____.

5. He gave the _____ to the _____.

6. Now the _____ has the _____.

7. Will the _____ read the _____?

8. The _____ read the _____, but not on the _____!

4. Double D Words

Teacher: "The word *dog* will fit in one space in each sentence below. One other word that also begins with *d* will fit in each of the other spaces. Complete the sentences."

1. _____ the _____ with the towel.

2. The towel will _____ the _____.

3. The _____ can _____ off in the sun.

4. Will the sun _____ the _____?

5. Keep the _____ _____ in winter.

5. More Double D Words

Teacher: "The word *dog* will fit in one blank space in each sentence below. Fill the other space with a word that begins with *d.*"

Example:

_____ said, "Where is the _____?"

   (Dad)   said, "Where is the   (dog)   ?"

1. The d_____ sat by the d_____.

2. The artist said, "I will d_____ a d_____.

3. The d_____ will d_____ the water.

4. D_____ the d_____ d_____ a hole in the yard?

5. Yes, the d_____ d_____ d_____ a hole in the yard!

Teacher: "Need a little help? These words fit the spaces: *dog, did, dig, drink, draw,* and *door.*"

6. Fun with Triple D Words

Teacher: "Each sentence has three missing words. Each missing word begins with the letter *d.* The words *dig, did,* and *dad* fit in each sentence. Where does each word fit?"

Example:

D _____ d_____ d_____ this hole?
    (Did)   (dad)   (dig)   this hole?

1. D_____ said he d_____ d_____ that hole.

2. D_____ d_____ d_____ the hole.

3. When d_____ d_____ d_____ that hole?

4. D_____ d_____ not d_____ the hole today.

INITIAL CONSONANT BLENDS

Consonant blends consist of two or more letters that are blended when pronouncing a word. If a child attempts to sound separately each of the consonants in a blend, distortion and confusion will result. These sounds must be blended to arrive at the correct pronunciation. Children know these speech sounds: They must learn to recognize their printed equivalents. For example, students know the sound of *s,* as heard in *see, sit, some,* and *say,* and the sound of *t,* as heard in *tell, to, talk,* and *top.* The next short step, from the known to the unknown, would be teaching the blend sound *st,* as heard in *stop, still, stand,* and the like.

Two- and three-letter consonant blends may be divided into three major groups on the basis of a common letter:

- Those in which *r* is the concluding letter (Column A)
- Those in which *l* is the concluding letter (Column B)
- Those that begin with the letter *s* (Column C)

A		B		C
br	scr	bl	spl	sc
cr	spr	cl		sk
dr	str	fl		sm
fr	thr	gl		sn
gr		pl		sp
pr		sl		st
tr				sw

The blends are listed alphabetically, but they may be taught in any order. The two-letter blends are easier to learn and occur more frequently in words met in beginning reading than do the three-letter blends; therefore, it is better to teach the two-letter blends first. See Table 5–3 for words that can be used in teaching consonant blends.

There are several ways to teach children how to master these blend sounds. Regardless of what approach you use, the objectives in teaching blends are to have children (a) see the letter combination involved; (b) realize that in every case the letters combine into a blend sound; and (c) discriminate between the blend sound and the sound of individual letters, as for example, in *pay, lay,* and *play.*

Procedures for teaching initial blends closely parallel those for teaching initial consonant sounds. To illustrate, we will look at the steps in teaching the sound represented by *st* in detail. All other consonant blends may be taught in the same manner.

● CHALKBOARD ACTIVITIES

Place a few *st* words on the board, such as *stop, still, star, stand,* and *stick.* Direct children's attention to the *st* beginning. As each word is pronounced, ask the students to listen to the *st* sound in initial position. Then invite the children to give other words that begin with the blended sounds *st* (*stone, step, stood, stir,* etc.).

● AUDITORY-VISUAL ASSOCIATION

1. Key Words (Two-letter Blends)
   a. Duplicate a series of key words that emphasize the common letter in a number of consonant blends, such as *r, l,* and *s.* Provide each child with a copy.
   b. Lead children in seeing and saying the blends and the key words in each column: *br* as in *bring, cr* as in *cry, dr* as in *drum.*

See the *r*		See the *l*		Begins with *s*	
br	*bring*	bl	*blue*	sc	*school*
cr	*cry*	cl	*clean*	sk	*sky*
dr	*drum*	fl	*fly*	sm	*small*
fr	*from*	gl	*glad*	sn	*snow*
gr	*green*	pl	*play*	sp	*spot*
pr	*pretty*	sl	*slow*	st	*stop*
tr	*tree*			sw	*swim*

2. Hearing Blends in Words (Identifying Blends Heard)
   a. Prepare columns showing three different blends.
   b. Pronounce a word that begins with one of the blends shown: "*bl*ue," "*st*and," "*tr*ain," and so on.
   c. Children underline the blend that is heard at the beginning of the stimulus word.

blue	*stand*	*train*	*play*	*smoke*
br	st	gl	pr	sn
pl	sl	tr	bl	sm
bl	sm	sk	pl	sp

TABLE 5–3 Words for Teaching Initial Consonant Blends

br	cr	dr	fr	gr	pr	tr
brother	cry	dress	friend	grade	pretty	tree
bring	cross	drink	from	great	present	train
brought	crop	draw	front	ground	president	trip
brown	creek	dry	Friday	green	program	truly
brake	crowd	drive	fruit	grandmother	print	trick
bread	cream	drop	fright	grass	produce	truck
bright	crack	dream	free	grandfather	prize	trade
bridge	crawl	drove	fresh	group	promise	trap
break	crib	drum	frog	grew	proud	track
brave	cried	drew	freeze	gray	product	true
brush	crumb	drill	frozen	grain	prepare	trail
branch	crown	drag	friendly	grab	protect	treat
brick	crow	drank	fry	grape	press	trim
broom	crook	drug	frost	grand	price	tramp

bl	cl	fl	pl	sl	sp	st
black	close	flower	play	sleep	spell	start
blue	clean	fly	place	sled	spend	stay
blow	class	floor	please	slid	spot	story
block	clothes	flag	plant	slate	speak	stop
bloom	climb	flew	plan	slip	spent	store
blew	club	flood	plane	slowly	sport	study
blanket	cloth	float	plenty	slave	speed	still
blood	cloud	flat	plain	slow	spoke	state
blackboard	clear	flour	plate	slipper	spirit	stand
blossom	clay		pleasant	slept	speech	stick
blind	clothing	*gl*	plow	sleet	spoon	stocking
blame	clock	glad	player	sleepy	spear	step
blizzard	climate	glass	plantation	slim	space	star
blaze	clown	glove	playmate	slick	spin	stood

sc	sk	sm	sn	sw	tw
school	skate	small	snow	swim	twelve
scare	skin	smoke	snake	sweet	twist
scold	sky	smell	snowball	swing	twenty
scout	ski	smile	snail	sweater	twice
scream	skip	smart	snap	swan	twin
schoolhouse	skirt	smooth	snug	sweep	twig
score	skunk	smack	sneeze	swell	twinkle

3. Word Recognition (Auditory-to-Visual Patterns)
a. Duplicate a number of three-word series as shown.
b. Pronounce one word from each series. (The stimulus word is italicized here, but would not be on hand-out material supplied to children.)
c. Children underline the word pronounced.

1	2	3	4	5
black	stay	smell	skin	*flew*
back	gay	*spell*	*sing*	few
brick	*gray*	sell	swing	true

6	7	8	9	10
snail	sin	dumb	grain	bake
scale	sink	*drum*	*rain*	*brake*
sail	*skin*	from	gain	rake

● PRINT AND SOUND

1. Add a Blend
Here the student writes the two letters that represent the initial blended sounds.
Teacher: "Write the letters that are shown above the blank spaces. Then pronounce the words you have made."

br	sp	cl	sw
_____ain	_____eak	_____ean	_____im
_____ake	_____oon	_____oth	_____eet
_____an	_____ace	_____ay	_____ay
_____own	_____in	_____imb	_____ell
_____ush	_____ell	_____ock	_____ing

2. Change a Blend
Use word endings that will make different words when different blends are added.
Teacher: "In each blank space write the blend shown on the left. Then pronounce each word."

(br) _____own	(sp) _____ill	(sk) _____ate
(cr) _____own	(st) _____ill	(pl) _____ate
(dr) _____own	(sk) _____ill	(st) _____ate
(fr) _____own	(dr) _____ill	(cr) _____ate
	(gr) _____ill	(sl) _____ate

● USING CONTEXT

Teacher: "Read the clue. Write a two-letter blend to make a word that goes with the clue."

Examples:

snake _____awls
(a snake *crawls*, so use *cr*)

fruit _____ and
(you can buy fruit at the fruit *stand*)
Note: All tasks in Set 1 begin with the same blend found in the clue. In Set 2 they are all different.

	Set 1		**Set 2**
Clue		*Clue*	
fresh	_____uit	snow	_____ake
tree	_____unk	broom	_____eeps
train	_____ack	scare	_____ow
brown	_____ead	draw	_____idge
sleds	_____ide	glue	_____icks
travel	_____ip	tree	_____ump

Teacher: "Read the clue. Complete the word that fits the clue. Use one of the blends *st, sp,* or *sn* to make a word that fits the clue."

Examples:

a place to buy	_____ore	use *st* to spell *store*
football, tennis	_____orts	use *sp* to spell *sports*

Clue		*Clue*	
1. hard metal	_____eel	**6.** to say something	_____eak
2. slow as a	_____ail	**7.** shines at night	_____ar
3. tops do this	_____in	**8.** sleep noise	_____ore
4. eat with this	_____oon	**9.** bees can	_____ing
5. to begin	_____art	**10.** as white as	_____ow

Teacher: "Write one of the blends *sl, sw,* or *sk* in the blank spaces to make a word that fits the clue."

Clue		*Clue*	
1. using a broom	_____eep	**6.** above the earth	_____y
2. women wear	_____irts	**7.** moves on snow	_____ed
3. not fast	_____ow	**8.** a beautiful fowl	_____an
4. very clever	_____y	**9.** arm goes in	_____eeve
5. a bunch of bees	_____arm	**10.** smells bad	_____unk

Teacher: "Write the blend that spells the word that fits the clue."

Examples:

pleased and happy   _____ad (gl)   train runs on it   _____ack (tr)

	Clue Box			
sl	tr	bl	cl	sp

1. near by   _____ose   **6.** to go up the hill   _____imb

2. close your eyes and   _____eep   **7.** runs on track   _____ain

3. what a top does   _____in   **8.** to say something   _____eak

4. cannot see   _____ind   **9.** a pretty color   _____ue

5. used to catch lobsters   _____ap   **10.** not very fast   _____ow

Teacher: "Read the clue. Write the word that fits the clue."

Example:

can write on this _____ (skate, *slate*)

      Clue

     1. food is placed on this   _____   (state, plate)

     2. not big or large   _____   (small, star)

     3. this jumps in the pond   _____   (frog, drop)

     4. not very far away   _____   (slow, close)

     5. what we do with a broom   _____   (sweep, speak)

Teacher: "How many *s*tudents can *s*tand on a *s*tump? Each of the following sentences has two missing words. The words *stand* and *stump* will fit in each sentence. Where does each word fit?"

Example:

Can you _____ on a _____?

Teacher: "This is easy; the context forces you to write: Can you *stand* on a *stump?* Finish the following sentences."

1. You can _____ on a _____.

2. A _____ can _____ in the woods.

3. A _____ can _____a long time.

4. We can both _____ on this large _____.

5. Can this _____ _____ for 50 years?

Teacher: "Since you are well *g*rounded in reading, it will be easy to *p*low through this exercise. Just *p*lant a few words in the blank spaces. Each sentence has two missing words. Two of the words *plow, plant,* or *ground* will fit in each sentence. Which two words fit where?"

Example:

After you _____ you can _____ crops.

Teacher: "When you use the context of the sentence, you will probably make it read: After you *plow* you can *plant* crops. Complete each of the following sentences using *plow*, *plant* or *ground*."

1. You must _____ the _____ in the spring.

2. Then you _____ seeds in the _____.

3. You must _____ before you _____.

4. Remember, _____ seeds after you _____.

5. Always prepare the _____ before you _____.

Teacher: "One of the letter clusters in the clue box will complete *all* the words in one sentence. Study each sentence and fill in the blanks."

Clue Box				
gr	cl	tr	st	dr

Example:

They _____ew many kinds of _____ain on the farm. (gr)

1. The _____own will _____ean the _____othes.

2. He _____ood ready to _____art telling the _____ory.

3. She did not _____op the _____um during the _____ill.

4. It was a _____eat to _____amp along the _____ail.

5. She _____ove to town to buy a _____ess.

Teacher: "John makes many speeches. The sentences that follow are all about John and his speeches. All blanks in these sentences are filled by one of these words:

speak   spoke   spoken   speaking   speaks   speaker

—Wait! The last word in the last sentence begins with a different blend."

1. John was invited to sp_____.

2. He is sp_____ now.

3. He will sp_____ again tomorrow.

4. He sp_____ twice this week.

5. He has sp_____many times this year.

6. He is a very good sp_____.

7. After he sp_____ he will eat a _____eak!

Initial Consonant Digraphs
(SH, WH, TH, AND CH)

A digraph is a combination of two letters that represent one speech sound. The sound heard is not a blend of the two letters involved, but a completely new sound. A given digraph may have more than one pronunciation, but the letter combination results in a single sound in each case (*ch* = *k* in *chorus; sh* in *chef; ch* in *church*). Digraphs may be taught in a similar way to that used for teaching consonant sounds.

Steps in Brief

1. Place several stimulus words on the chalkboard: *shall, she, ship,* and *show.*
2. Ask the children to look at the words carefully and note how they are alike. Draw out the observation that all the words begin with *sh.* (Underline the digraph being taught: *sh, ch, th,* or *wh.*)
3. Ask the children to listen to the sound of *sh* as they say the words together.
4. Invite children to supply other words that begin with the same sound as *shall, she, ship,* and *show.*

Note: The digraph *sh* usually has the sound heard in these stimulus words. Other common *sh* words are *shut, shop, shot, sheep, shape, shade, short, sheet, shoot, shoe, shell, shirt, shovel, shake, sharp,* and *shine.*

The digraph *wh* is usually pronounced as if spelled *hw:* when = hwen; white = hwite. The *wh* sound may be taught as *sh* was above, with *when, white, what,* and *which* as stimulus words. Other common *wh* words are *why, where, wheel, wheat, whisper, whether, whale,* and *whiskers.* Exceptions: When *o* follows *wh,* the *w* is silent, as in who = hōō; whole = hōl; whom = hōōm; whose = hōōz. (Changing patterns of pronunciation have likely caused some dictionaries to recognize a second pronunciation: when = wĕn.)

The digraph *th* has two common sounds. There is the voiced *th* sound as in *this, their, they, though, that, then, there, than,* and *them,* and the unvoiced *th* sound as in *thing, thin, thimble, thank, think, thick, third,* and *thumb.* (The concepts of voiced and unvoiced need not be taught in relation to reading.)

While the consonant digraph *ch* has three different sounds, the most common and the one met almost exclusively in beginning reading is that of *ch* heard in *chair* or *chop.* Common words for use in teaching *ch* exercises include the following:

chair	chin	chose	charm	chalk
child	check	chop	chance	cheer
chicken	cheek	change	chimney	chief

Much later, children will meet the other sounds represented by *ch.* These need not be taught in beginning reading.

ch = k		*ch = sh*	
chorus	(kō rus)	chef	(shef)
character	(kar ak ter)	chassis	(shas ē)
chemist	(kem ist)	chauffeur	(sho fur)

choir	(kwir)	chic	(shēk)
chord	(kord)	chiffon	(shif on)
chrome	(krom)	chamois	(sham ē)

Blends in Sentence Context

Prepare a number of sentences in which a high percentage of the words begin with the digraphs *sh*, *ch*, *wh*, and *th*. These may be presented via the chalkboard, transparencies, or duplicated worksheets. After reading the material silently, children volunteer to read a sentence to the group.

1. Charles and Chip chatted in the church chapel.
2. Chester chose a chunk of cheese and some chips from the chest.
3. Shirley showed the shells to Sherman.
4. The shepherd sheltered the sheep in the shadow of the shed.
5. His white whiskers were whirled by the whistling wind.
6. Mr. White whispered when and where the whale would appear.
7. On Thursday, Thelma thought of thirty things to do.
8. Thad thought about a thorn in his thumb.

● USING CONTEXT

Teacher: "Read the clue word. Following each clue, complete a word that has the opposite meaning. Use one of the digraphs *ch, th, sh,* or *wh* to do this."

Example:

pride _____ame (write *sh* for *shame*)

	Clue			Clue	
1. adult	_____ild		**6.** dull	_____arp	
2. tall	_____ort		**7.** retreat	_____arge	
3. open	_____ut		**8.** freeze	_____aw	
4. fat	_____in		**9.** thin	_____ick	
5. shout	_____isper		**10.** warm	_____illy	

Teacher: "Read the clue. Build a word, using *ch, sh, th,* or *wh,* that fits the clue."

Example:

can dig with this _____ovel (sh)

	Clue	
1. fits on foot	_____oe	
2. not very tall	_____ort	
3. round and rolls	_____eel	
4. speaking very softly	_____isper	
5. writes on blackboard	_____alk	

6. leader of the tribe _____ief

7. one on each hand _____umb

8. after first and second _____ird

9. we sit on this _____air

10. found on the beach _____ell

Teacher: "Each sentence shows two words containing blank spaces. One digraph, *ch, sh, th,* or *wh,* will fit the blanks in both words. Study each sentence and complete each word."

Example:

Don't let the (*ch*)icken eat the (*ch*)alk.

1. The _____eep were resting in the _____ade.

2. Who put the _____alk mark on the _____air?

3. _____ich of the _____eels is broken?

4. He bought a _____irt in the _____op.

5. She had a _____imble on her _____umb.

6. After a purchase, always _____eck your _____ange.

● FUN WITH LANGUAGE

Teacher: "Each sentence below contains some incomplete words. A digraph, *ch, th, sh,* or *wh,* is missing in each word. Read the clue box carefully and then complete the sentences."

Clue Box

Chuck and Sue plan to go shopping.

Knowing this will help you.

Remember, the missing parts are *ch, th, sh,* or *wh*.

---

1. Sue said, "_____ere _____all we _____op?"

2. _____uck said, "And _____at _____all we buy?"

3. I _____ink we _____ould _____eck the ads," said _____uck.

4. _____en I will _____op for _____oes and a _____irt.

5. Sue wanted to _____op for _____ite _____oes.

6. I _____ink _____ey _____ould have fun _____ile _____opping!

● THE *WH* ROUNDUP

Teacher: Tease out the meaning. In the following sentences, each unfinished word begins with *wh. Wh*ich word goes *wh*ere? All sentences are based on the clue box.

> *Clue Box*
> "Sam lives in a white house on Whale Street."

Finish each word so that it makes sense in the sentence.

1. Wh_____ house on Wh_____ Street is Sam's house?

2. Sam lives on Wh_____ Street in a wh_____ house.

3. Sam, wh_____ house is wh_____, lives on Wh_____ Street.

4. Wh_____ house is the wh_____ house wh_____ Sam lives?

5. Wh_____ on Wh_____ Street is Sam's wh_____ house?

6. Wh_____ did Sam move into the wh_____ house?

FINAL CONSONANTS, BLENDS, AND DIGRAPHS

Some of the procedures for teaching initial sounds can be adapted to teaching final sounds. The teaching objective remains the same—to help children visually recognize letter forms and associate these with the sounds they represent in words.

1. Chalkboard Drill
   a. Select the letter-sound to be taught.
   b. Place stimulus words on the board.
   c. Call children's attention to the final letter.
   d. Pronounce each word carefully, so that children hear the sound at the end of the word.
   e. Have children pronounce words and supply others that end with the sound.

2. Print and Sound
   a. Prepare columns of easy words, all of which end with a particular letter-sound.
   b. Omit the final letter.
   c. Children print the letter indicated and pronounce the word.

Add d	*Add* n	*Add* p	*Add* g	*Add* t
sa__	gu__	li__	ho__	ne__
mu__	wi__	ca__	pi__	hu__
ha__	te__	na__	ta__	co__
ro__	ru__	cu__	wi__	hi__

Variations:

Add one of the letters *m, x,* or *b* to make a word. Pronounce each word.

bo__	gu__	ro__	dru__	fo__
roo__	mi__	ha__	gra__	so__
hi__	tu__	si__	wa__	ta__

Change the last letter of words in the first column so that the new word names something living.

Examples:

pin	pi__	(g)	pig
plane	plan__	(t)	plant

1. but	bu__		**6.** map	ma__
2. lamp	lam__		**7.** dot	do__
3. fog	fo__		**8.** hem	he__
4. call	cal__		**9.** owe	ow__
5. cap	ca__		**10.** sharp	shar__

● USING CONTEXT

Teacher: "Finish each of the following sentences so that it makes sense. Put the letter *m* or *n* in each blank space. You must read carefully to know which letter fits into which blank."

Example:

Pa__had a talk with a ma__.

Teacher: " 'Pan had a talk with a mam' makes no sense. The sentence 'Pam had a talk with a man' is correct. Remember that every blank has to be filled with *m* or *n*."

1. Sa__can count to te__.

2. Ca__you see the me__?

3. She gave hi__a stick of gu__.

4. Please pass the ha__.

5. Mo__put ja__on the bu__.

The purpose of the following exercise is to provide practice in hearing the letter sounds *p, d,* and *b* at the end of words.

Teacher: "Finish each sentence below so that it makes sense. Put one of the letters *b, d,* or *p* in each blank space. You must read carefully to know which letter fits in each space."

Example:
A baby bear is a cu___. (can't be cup or cud)
A baby bear is a cub.

Set 1

1. Turn on the lam___.

2. They rode in a taxi ca___.

3. He took a short na___.

4. I like corn on the co___.

5. A bee stung him on the han___.

Set 2

1. Bo___plays in the ban___.

2. The guide said, "Here is the ma___."

3. The water in the tu___was col___.

4. Di___he leave his ca___in the ca___?

5. Mother said, "Gra___the pu___."

The following are some stimulus words to use in board or seatwork exercises:

b	d	f	g	k (ck)	l (ll)	m
Bob	sad	if	dog	back	call	him
tub	fed	calf	big	rock	tell	room
club	send	muff	flag	black	hill	gum
grab	glad	stiff	rug	trick	pull	ham
rob	cold	puff	drug	duck	still	whom
rib	band	off	bag	pick	small	drum

n	p	r	s (s)	s (=z)	t
can	hop	for	bus	his	cat
win	cap	star	yes	as	met
men	stop	her	dress	ours	shut
thin	up	dear	us	is	hit
when	step	door	less	has	set
ran	skip	clear	likes	runs	sat
moon	map	car	miss	days	but

Consonant Digraphs *ch, sh,* and *th* at the End of Words

The sounds of the digraphs *ch, sh,* and *th* will have been taught already because they occur at the beginning of words. Procedures for teaching these sounds at the end of words may parallel those used for teaching initial sounds.

1. Place stimulus words on the board.

2. Have the children look at the letter combinations under discussion.

3. Pronounce each word carefully so children hear the sound at the end of the word.

4. Have the children pronounce the words.

Other stimulus words ending with *ch, sh,* or *th* are *March, church, peach, branch, ditch, search, teach, patch, bench; fish, cash, fresh, rush, crash, dish, flash, wish, push; both, bath, tenth, north, health, path, length, fifth,* and *cloth.*

● USING CONTEXT

Teacher: "Read the clue word. Complete the word that follows, using one of the digraphs *ch, sh,* or *th.*

Clue Word		Clue Word	
fruit	pea_____	vegetable	squa_____
two	bo_____	direction	nor_____
month	Mar_____	meal	lun_____
money	ca_____	insect	mo_____
lightning	fla_____	wreck	cra_____
trail	pa_____	worship	chur_____

Teacher: "Some language games are easier than they look! To complete the following sentences you must write one of the digraphs *ch, sh,* or *th* in each blank space. Reading the rest of the sentence makes it easy."

Example:

Eat fre_____ fi_____ for your heal_____.

Teacher: "The only way for the sentence to make sense is by using *ch, sh,* or *th* in the three blanks. Remember, either *ch, sh,* or *th* will fit in each blank."

1. "Are the fi_____ fre_____?" he asked.

2. Bo_____ nor_____ and sou_____ are directions.

3. A bran_____ fell from the pea_____ tree.

4. The parade will mar_____ down the pa_____.

5. Whi_____ clo_____ needs the pat_____?

6. We had fre_____ fi_____ for lun_____.

7. Mar_____ is the third mon_____.

Consonant Digraphs *nk, ng,* and *ck* at the End of Words

Teaching *nk, ng,* and *ck* involves associating these letter combinations at the end of words or syllables with the sounds they represent. These digraphs may be taught by instructing children that, for example, "The sound of *nk* at the end of words is the sound we hear in these words:"

bank	link	junk
rank	mink	sunk
sank	pink	drunk
tank	sink	shrunk

Other words to use in board or seatwork exercises include *ink, blink, drink, think; plank, drank, spank, frank; trunk, chunk,* and *bunk.*

"The sound of *ng* at the end of words is the sound we hear in these words:"

bang	king	gong	hung
gang	ring	bong	rung
hang	wing	strong	sprung
sang	sing	song	sung

"The letters *ck* have the sound of *k.* Listen to the sound at the end of these words:"

back	pick	dock	luck
pack	kick	lock	duck
sack	sick	block	truck
crack	trick	sock	buck

Final Consonant Blends (*st, sk, ld, mp,* and *nd*)

Teaching procedures described throughout this chapter can be used or adapted to teach blended consonants occurring at the end of words (*st, sk, ld, mp,* and *nd*):

mu*st*	a*sk*	co*ld*	ju*mp*	fi*nd*
fa*st*	de*sk*	wi*ld*	ca*mp*	ba*nd*
re*st*	ma*sk*	fie*ld*	du*mp*	fou*nd*
mo*st*	du*sk*	chi*ld*	cha*mp*	be*nd*

CONSONANT IRREGULARITIES

Fortunately, sounds represented by consonant letters involve less variability than is found in vowel letter-sounds. Nevertheless, a number of consonants and consonant combinations result in pronunciation irregularities that must be taught. The majority of these fall into one of the following groupings:

- Consonants that have more than one sound (for example, c sounded as k or s; g sounded as g or j; and s sounded as s, z, sh, or zh)
- Consonants that are not sounded (know, light, wrap)
- Consonant combinations with unique pronunciations (ph = f; que = k)

The Two Sounds of c (k and s)

The letter c represents no distinctive sound of its own. It is sounded as k when followed by the vowels a, o, and u and as s when followed by i, e, or y. The hard (k) sound occurs most frequently and for this reason is usually taught first. Eight words on the Dolch List begin with the letter c, and in all of these the letter has its k sound. Only 4 of the 58 words on the Dale List that begin with c have the s sound. Chalkboard and duplicated seatwork exercises can provide drill as needed. Here are some examples:

c is sounded k when followed by	a	o	u
	call	cold	cut
	cake	come	cup
	care	coat	cute
	cap	cook	cub
c is sounded s when followed by	i	e	y
	city	cent	cymbal
	cinder	cement	cypress
	cider	mice	cynic
	citizen	voice	cylinder

Some words include both sounds of c: circle, cycle, and circus.
Teacher: "Say each word softly aloud, then on each blank space write s or k to show the sound of the letter c."

__ cat	__ comb	__ ceiling	__ color
__ center	__ citizen	__ cuff	__ cellar

The Two Sounds of g (g and j)

1. The letter g has its regular (hard) sound when followed by a, u, and o.
2. The letter g is often sounded as j when followed by i, e, and y. (Common exceptions: *give, girl, get, geese,* and *gift.*)

Dealing with the two sounds of *g* is not so much a matter of teaching but of simply acquainting children with this phenomenon. Only a few words are met in beginning reading in which *g* is sounded as *j*. After stating the two rules, children may practice hearing the two sounds.

Teacher: "Pronounce each word softly, then on each blank space write *g* or *j* to show the sound that *g* represents."

__ George	__ goat	__ gem	__ game
__ gum	__ giant	__ gave	__ gentle
__ garden	__ general	__ gold	__ gun

Sounds Represented by the Letter *s*

1. The letter *s* usually represents its regular sound as heard in *said, set, sing, soap,* and *sun.*
2. The letter *s* is sometimes sounded as *z* when it is the final sound in the word: *is, his, has, ours, please, cheese,* and *noise.*
3. The letter *s* is sounded *sh* in *sure* and *sugar.*
4. The letter *s* is sounded *zh* in *measure* and *treasure.*

It is highly doubtful that the irregularities associated with the letter *s* have any significant impact on learning to read.

Consonants Not Sounded

A large number of English words contain one or more letters that are not sounded. In some instances, particularly when the initial letter is not sounded, it pays to learn the words as sight words. Instant word recognition and independent reading are enhanced by deliberately calling to children's attention the more frequently occurring instances of consonants that are not sounded. We can make the following generalizations:

1. In words containing double consonants, the first is sounded, the second is not.
2. In words beginning with *kn*, the *k* is usually not sounded.
3. The combination *gh* is usually not sounded when preceded by the vowel *i.*
4. In words beginning with *wr,* the *w* is usually not sounded.
5. In words ending with the syllable *-ten*, the *t* is often not sounded.
6. The digraph *ck* is pronounced as *k.*
7. In words ending with *mb*, the *b* is usually not sounded.

It is doubtful that learning these rules in isolation or as a series of generalizations has virtue. Working with a series of stimulus words that follow one or more of the rules will help children gain insight into the pronunciation of words. Table 5–4 provides examples of words that follow each of these seven generalizations.

While a given generalization may be introduced in a particular grade, it will probably have to be reviewed in subsequent grades. For some children, simple review will not be adequate, and the generalization and applications will have to be retaught. By means of close observation or diagnosis, the teacher—at any grade level—discovers

TABLE 5–4 Consonants Not Sounded

Double Consonants	kn Words	gh Words	wr Words	-ten Ending	-ck Ending	-mb Ending
ladder	know	sigh	write	often	sack	comb
collect	knee	light	wring	soften	neck	thumb
fellow	knight	sight	wrote	listen	block	climb
message	knew	bright	wrap	hasten	kick	bomb
roller	knit	flight	wrath	fasten	duck	lamb
summer	knife	night	wrist	glisten	clock	plumb
dinner	knock	might	wrong	moisten	black	limb
yellow	kneel	slight	wren	brighten	trick	numb
happen	knob	blight	wreck	tighten	back	crumb
kitten	known	right	wreath	frighten	pick	dumb

which children need help on a particular skill and can work individually with these children or devise seatwork exercises that provide practice in the areas in which deficiencies are noted. Words of appropriate difficulty can be selected for use in various types of teaching exercises. The difficulty level of the exercises can be further controlled by the task or tasks the children are called upon to perform.

The purpose of the following exercises is to explain the concept that some letters in words may not represent a sound. At this level, one need not explain in the language of linguistic science. The term *silent letters* is inaccurate, since no letters make sounds; however, to use this term with 6-year-olds is not poor pedagogy.

1. *Directions:* Place material on the chalkboard similar to the examples in the box. Pronounce each word. Call attention to the pair of like consonants and the fact that they represent one sound. Draw a slash through the second consonant in each pair to indicate that it is not sounded.

> summer dress letter bell
> Two like consonants stand for one sound.
> letter summer dress bell

Put words on the chalkboard that illustrate this concept or duplicate material for seatwork. Have children cross out the letter that is not sounded.

dinner	kitten	tall
glass	cuff	barrel
ball	ladder	yellow
hidden	doll	fuzz
cross	grass	sudden
rabbit	happen	class

2. *Purpose:* To provide practice in sight recognition of words that contain one or more of the irregular spellings *kn, wr, igh, mb, ph = f,* and *gh = f.*

Directions: Explain the irregularities of the letter combinations discussed. Have the children note that the words in each line contain the letter pattern shown on the left. Have them practice pronouncing each word and learn these words as sight words.

kn: knew known knee knight knit knock know
(the *k* is not sounded)

wr: write wrong wreck wrote wring wrap wrist
(the *w* is not sounded)

igh: light night sight bright right fight might
(*i* = ī; *gh* is not sounded)

mb: comb lamb thumb climb crumb bomb
(the final letter *b* is not sounded)

ph: phone photo nephew phonics autograph phrase
(*ph* represents the sound of *f*)

gh: laugh cough rough enough tough laughter
(final letters represent the sound of *f*)

3. *Directions:* Have the children read the following sentences softly aloud to themselves, then underline the letters *kn, wr, ph, gh,* and *mb* each time they appear in a word.

1. The knight knew how to write so he wrote a pamphlet.
2. He took a right turn on the wrong light and had a wreck.
3. The wreck was quite a sight in the bright moonlight.
4. Phil hurt his knee and thumb taking photographs that night.
5. If you know the alphabet and phonics you can learn to read and write.

4. *Teacher:* "Pronounce all the words in each A column. Then strike out each silent consonant in the words in the A columns. The first one is done for you. In the space under B, write the dictionary pronunciation of each word." (This will be used later in conjunction with dictionary work.)

A	B	A	B
si~~gh~~t	sīt	~~k~~ni~~gh~~t	_____
hasten	_____	glisten	_____
knew	_____	comb	_____
rabbit	_____	right	_____
thick	_____	write	_____
climb	_____	black	_____
wrote	_____	funnel	_____
dollar	_____	known	_____

debt	_____	doubt	_____
knock	_____	truck	_____
soften	_____	often	_____
summer	_____	tunnel	_____
sigh	_____	thumb	_____

5. The following exercise illustrates that unsounded letters are useful in that they produce a different word that has the same pronunciation but a different meaning from the word to which the unsounded letter is added. This letter provides a visual clue to the meaning of the new word.

Teacher: "In column B, add a letter that is not sounded to each word in column A in order to produce a different word."

A	B	A	B
new	_____	night	_____
hole	_____	be	_____
our	_____	cent	_____
rap	_____	not	_____
nob	_____	plum	_____
in	_____	ring	_____

qu and *que* Combinations (*kw* and *k*)

Qu The letter *q* has no sound of its own and is always followed by *u,* which in this case does not function as a vowel. The combination *qu* is pronounced *kw,* as in *quick* = *kw*ik and *quack* = *kw*ak.

Other *qu* words that might be used in teaching exercises include *queen, quart, quiet, quit, Quaker, quake, quite, quarter, quail,* and *quarrel.*

Que *Que* at the end of words has the sound of *k;* usually *que* is blended with the preceding syllable:

picturesque = pĭk chûr ĕsk	plaque = plăk
antique = ăn tēk	grotesque = grō tĕsk
burlesque = bûr lĕsk	clique = klēk
opaque =ō pāk	brusque = brŭsk
critique = krĭ tēk	technique = tĕk nēk

Note that the final syllable in *que* words is accented.

SUMMARY

In this chapter we built on children's previously acquired skills of auditory-visual discrimination and dealt with teaching consonant letter-sound relationships. There is a good rationale for teaching consonants in initial position in words. You now have steps for teaching single letters, blends (clusters), and digraphs, and suggestions for helping children master certain consonant letter-sound irregularities.

In general, consonant letters are quite consistent in the sounds they represent. Letters that represent only one sound include *b, d, h, j, k, l, m, n, p, r, w,* and initial *y.*

Consonants that combine include the following:

- *Consonant blends* (clusters), in which two or more letters blend so that sound elements of each letter are heard: *bl, bl*ack; *str, str*ing; *spl, spl*ash; and *gl, gl*ide.
- *Consonant digraphs,* in which two-letter combinations result in one speech sound that is not a blend of the letters involved: *sh*all; *wh*ite; *th*is (voiced *th*); *th*ink (unvoiced *th*); *ch*air; *ch*orus (*ch* = *k*); and *ch*ef (*ch* = *sh*).

Some consonants and consonant combinations have irregular spellings:

Unsounded Consonants in Specific Combinations

1. The *k* is not sounded in *kn* (k̸new, k̸nee)
2. Double consonants—only one is sounded (sum̸mer)
3. When the vowel *i* precedes *gh,* the latter is not sounded (lig̸h̸t)
4. The *w* is not sounded in *wr* at the beginning of words (w̸riting)
5. When a word ends with the syllable *-ten,* the *t* is often not sounded (oft̸en, fast̸en)
6. The *ck* combination is pronounced *k* (sac̸k, cloc̸k)
7. The *b* is not sounded in *mb* at the end of words (comb̸, lamb̸)

There are two sounds for the consonant *c:*

1. *c* = *k* in *cake, corn,* and *curl*
2. *c* = *s* when followed by *i, e,* or *y* (*city, cent, cinder*)

There are two sounds for the consonant *g:*

1. regular sound in *go, game,* and *gum*
2. *g* = *j* when followed by *e* or *i* (*gem,* giant)

Other irregularities include the following:

1. *ph* = *f* (*photo* = *foto; graph* = *graf*)
2. *qu* = *kw* (*quack* = *kwack*). The letter *q* has no sound of its own. In English spellings, *q* is always followed by the letter *u.*
3. The letter *s* may be sounded in a number of ways.
   a. *s* = *s* (most common) (*sell, soft, said*)
   b. *s* = *z* (*his* = *hiz; runs* = *runz*)
   c. *s* = *sh* (*sugar*)
   d. *s* = *zh* (*treasure*)

6

VOWEL LETTER-SOUND RELATIONSHIPS

Teaching the vowel letter-sound relationships is undoubtedly the most difficult and confusing part of an entire phonics program. This stems from two factors:

1. The variability of the sounds that vowels represent.
2. The tendency to overteach certain vowel letter-sound relationships, which can be confusing rather than helpful.

We have already discussed the variability of vowel letter-sounds in Chapter 1; in essence, all the rules or generalizations that have been advanced to cover vowel letter-sounds turn out to have numerous exceptions. Nevertheless, to be successful in the decoding process, children must develop insights relative to the relationship between visual letter patterns and the sounds these patterns *usually* represent. The apparent variability in spelling and sounds should point up the fact that a number of high-frequency words should be learned as sight words. A list of these sight words is provided in Table 6–1 at the end of this chapter.

PHONICS INSTRUCTION AS OVERKILL

The second problem in teaching vowel letter-sound relationships stems from the fact that teachers and schools sometimes forget the limited purpose of phonics instruction in the learning-to-read process (see Figure 6–1). The issues are Do we teach some "phonics" that has relatively little impact on learning to read? and Do we overteach some facets of letter-sound relationships that are more appropriate for producing junior linguists rather than beginning readers?

When our goal is simply teaching children to read, some minute differences in letter-sounds need not be dealt with at all. Certain other differences can be pointed out without forcing children to spend time discriminating these sounds in lists of words. What we sometimes forget in dealing with native speakers of English is that children can pronounce and thus differentiate among words that contain different sound values for a

FIGURE 6–1 The cartoonist Malcolm Hancock suggests that phonics can be overtaught as he shows an artistic disdain for vowels.

given vowel, such as *a* in *almost, loyal, path, idea,* and *father.* Furthermore, when children are reading for meaning, the problem diminishes in importance.

SEQUENCE IN TEACHING VOWEL LETTER-SOUNDS

There are certain factors relating to the sequence of teaching skills that have served as the basis for lengthy debate. Many of these may be of little importance to children learning to read; which vowel letter-sound to teach first, whether to teach short or long sounds first, or whether to teach these two sounds concomitantly are probably not crucial issues. In fact, a quite reasonable rationale could be made for opposite views pertaining to most matters of sequence.

In advocating the teaching of short vowel sounds first, it can be pointed out that a majority of the words children meet in beginning reading contain short vowel sounds. Many of these words are single-vowel-in-medial-position words. The phonic generalization for this situation, one vowel in medial position usually has its short sound, applies in a large percentage of words met in beginning reading.

Advocacy of teaching long vowel sounds first rests on the fact that the vowel name is the long sound of the vowel (*a, e, i, o, u*). It is frequently suggested that this fact makes it easy to teach the letter-sound association.

SHORT VOWEL SOUNDS

The generalizations that cover short vowel sounds deal primarily with initial single vowels and single vowels in medial position in words. Both of these vowel situations can be covered by the statement, "A single vowel that does not conclude a word usually has its short sound"; for example, *am, an, and, ant, as, ask, at,* and *act.*

The vast majority of words covered have a vowel in medial position, however, and as a result, the following generalization is used more frequently: "A single vowel in medial position usually has its short sound," as we see when we add an initial consonant to the words for the first generalization: *ham, can, hand, pant, gas, task, bat,* and *fact.*

We will illustrate methods for teaching the short vowel sound in medial position. To avoid repetition, we will use a teaching procedure to illustrate only one vowel sound; however, any of the approaches described can be used to teach each of the other vowel letter-sounds that fit the generalization. You will also find brief word lists for teaching each of the vowel letter-sounds.

For the short sound of *a* (ă), explain to children that they have learned the sounds the consonants represent in words and that they will now practice hearing one of the sounds represented by the vowel *a:*

> Teacher: "When we say the name of the vowel letter, we hear what is called the vowel's long sound.
> "Today we are going to listen carefully and learn to hear another sound for the vowel *a*—its short sound. I am going to put some words on the board. We have studied these words before. Each of the words has the letter *a* in it. Listen to the sound the *a* has in each word."

Begin by writing these words on the chalkboard: *man, had, back, ran, cap,* and *tag.*

1. Pronounce each word, moving your hand from left to right through the word.
2. Emphasize the sound of *a* in each word, but do not distort the sound.
3. Have the children say the words in unison, asking them to listen for the sound of ă.
4. Stress that the sound heard is called the short sound of *a.* Have the children note how this sound differs from the letter name.
5. Ask students how many vowels they see in each word and where the vowel is located (middle of the word).
6. Have children state what sound is heard when there is one vowel in the middle of a word.[1]
7. Have children state in their own words the rule that covers this vowel situation.

Using this approach, the following generalization will evolve: "One vowel in the middle of the word usually has its short sound." It is probably not essential that each child be able to recite all the generalizations in this chapter. At this point, it might be profitable to cite other familiar words that follow the generalizations under discussion, even though all the stimulus words are not yet known as sight words.

---

[1]Strictly speaking, the vowel in words such as *back, bank,* and *trap* is not in the middle of the word. Children are usually not confused by this statement, but you can modify the generalization if you wish.

Using Word Families

Some teachers find that certain children can do better in fixing the short sound of a given vowel if they see and pronounce a series of words that contain larger identical units than the vowel alone: the words *big, ship, tin,* and *hill* have an identical unit— *i.* The words *big, pig, dig,* and *fig;* and *hill, fill, bill,* and *pill;* and *sit, fit, bit,* and *kit* have rhyming units composed of several letters that have precisely the same phonic value in each word. Word families can be used both for teaching common phonic elements and for rapid recognition as sight words.

To teach the phonogram *ad,* you might begin with these words: *dad, had, sad, mad, bad,* and *lad.* Use the seven steps previously outlined to teach this and other identical phonogram words.

1. Pronounce each word; have children pronounce the words.
2. Stress the vowel sound heard and the visual pattern: one vowel, medial position.

Sample words follow for the vowels *e, i, o,* and *u.* The first column under each vowel includes words with mixed initial and final consonants; the second column presents the same final phonogram (letter-pattern) in each word.

e		*i*		*o*		*u*	
red	jet	big	hit	hop	cot	bus	bug
let	pet	tin	bit	job	not	run	rug
bell	let	hill	sit	stop	hot	cup	hug
send	bet	did	pit	log	pot	jump	jug
men	met	pig	fit	box	got	cut	mug
step	set	lift	lit	rock	lot	must	tug

● **USING CONTEXT**

Teacher: "Read the clue. Use one of the vowel letters *a, e,* or *o* to spell the word that fits the clue."

Example:
Clue
spider   w__b   use *e* to spell *web*
angry   m__d   use *a* to spell *mad*
horses   tr__t   use *o* to spell *trot*

	Clue			Clue	
1.	fishing	n__t	**6.**	soda	p__p
2.	chicken	h__n	**7.**	number	t__n
3.	steal	r__b	**8.**	floor	l__mp
4.	bird's	n__st	**9.**	cry	s__b
5.	paper	b__g	**10.**	lion's	d__n

Teacher: "Use one of the vowel letters *i, u,* or *e* to spell the word."

	Clue			*Clue*	
1.	chewy	g__m	**6.**	fish	sw___m
2.	color	r__d	**7.**	scissors	c__t
3.	tops	sp__n	**8.**	rings	b__ll
4.	plane	j__t	**9.**	fruit	pl__m
5.	ruler	k__ng	**10.**	large	b__g

Teacher: "Read the clue. Write the vowel that completes the word that fits the clue."

Example:

you sleep on this   b__d   (e)

Clue				
it's large	b__g	can ring it	b__ll
paper sack	b__g	can throw it	b__ll
an insect	b__g	lives on a farm	b__ll
to keep asking for	b__g	a boy's name	B__ll

Teacher: "Read the clue. Write the word that fits the clue."

Example:

The pig is in the _____.   (pin, pen)

Clue

Do you like corn on the _____?	(cab, cob)
John said, "I can read the _____."	(mop, map)
The cat drank milk from the _____.	(cap, cup)
Cats and dogs are _____.	(pots, pets)
A baby bear is a _____.	(cab, cub)

Teacher: "Each sentence has two blanks. One of the words *pig* or *pen* will fit in each space. Study each sentence and write the correct words."

Example:

The (*pig*) is in the (*pen*).

1. Put the _____ in the _____.

2. Will the _____ hold the _____?

3. The _____ will hold the _____.

4. The _____ should be in the _____.

5. The _____ is for the _____.

6. Is the _____ in the _____?

7. The _____ belongs in the _____.

8. It is time to _____ up the _____.

Teacher: "Read each sentence. One of the words at the right fits in the blank space. The only difference in the words is the vowel letter. Write the correct word in the blank space."

Example:

The _____ was many years old.	click clock
1. There was a _____ on the beach.	crab crib
2. The _____ was full of coal.	trick truck
3. John was able to _____ the word.	spell spill
4. Spot is a _____ dog.	smell small
5. _____ the letter in the mailbox.	Drop Drip

● FUN WITH LANGUAGE

Teacher: "Fill every blank space with a vowel. The context will help you pick the right vowel."
Clue: Suzy sings a lot.
Will she sing a song again if she has just sung that song?

1. Just ask Suzy and she will s__ng any s__ng.
2. Once she s__ng a very pretty s__ng.
3. Later, someone asked her to s__ng that s__ng again.
4. She said, "I just s__ng that s__ng."
5. I should not s__ng a s__ng that I have just s__ng.
6. Was Suzy right not to s__ng that s__ng again?
7. Would you s__ng a s__ng you had just s__ng?
8. If you have just s__ng a s__ng and you want to s__ng it again, s__ng it!

● BUCKETS AND BLANK SPACES

Teacher: "Note that each word with a blank in it has the same three letters. To complete each word you must add a vowel. Which vowel goes where? As you read the sentence, the context will indicate where to add *a, e, i,* and *u.*"

1. First, you f__ll the bucket f__ll of water.
2. Don't f__ll while carrying a bucket f__ll of water.

3. If you f__ll, the bucket might not be f__ll.

4. He f__ll, then he had to f__ll the bucket again.

5. Don't f__ll if you want a f__ll bucket.

Teacher: "In each of the following sentences, two words need a vowel. The context will help you decide which words fit. Write the vowel letter to complete each word."

Set 1

Use only the vowels *u, i,* and *e.*

1. Is the b__g very b__g?

2. S__t the basket down and come s__t by me.

3. Don't d__g where we d__g yesterday.

4. That t__n cup cost t__n cents.

5. She asked h__m, "Can you h__m this song?"

6. You write with a p__n, not with a p__n.

Set 2

Use only the vowels *a, o,* and *i.*

1. The c__t was asleep on the c__t.

2. "Watch out," said Joe, "the p__t is very h__t."

3. I want to s__t where we s__t yesterday.

4. Ask h__m if he wants a h__m sandwich.

5. Put the b__g dish in the paper b__g.

6. When the weather is h__t you should wear a h__t.

Minimal Contrast Vowels

Practice in associating vowel letter forms with the short sounds they represent can be presented in many ways. The examples start with contrasting two vowel sounds and gradually move through all vowels in medial position.

Contrasting two vowel sounds. As soon as two vowel sounds have been introduced, the difference between them can be stressed.

1. Write pairs of words on the chalkboard:

bat—bet	mat—met	pat—pet	sat—set
man—men	tan—ten	bad—bed	lad—led

2. Pronounce these words, inviting children to listen to the difference in the vowel sounds heard in the middle of the words.

3. Have children pronounce the pairs of words, noting each vowel letter form and the sound it represents.

The short sounds of *e* and *i* often pose special difficulty because of either poor auditory discrimination or dialectical differences in pronunciation. The following pairs of words, identical except for the vowel *i* or *e*, can be used in both auditory and visual drill:

led—lid	big—beg	pig—peg	wit—wet
pin—pen	tin—ten	din—den	met—mitt
bed—bid	pep—pip	bet—bit	rid—red
lit—let	pit—pet	sit—set	hem—him

Various exercises using different modes of presentation can be built from pairs of words such as these:

u, i	*u, e*	*a, u*	*o, u*
bug—big	bug—beg	bag—bug	cot—cut
but—bit	but—bet	bat—but	hot—hut
hut—hit	nut—net	cat—cut	not—nut
dug—dig	hum—hem	cap—cup	hog—hug

e, o	*a, o*	*a, i*	*i, o*
get—got	cat—cot	lap—lip	hip—hop
let—lot	hat—hot	nap—nip	tip—top
net—not	pat—pot	rap—rip	Tim—Tom
pet—pot	rat—rot	tap—tip	hit—hot

Seeing and sounding drill. After all short vowel letter-sounds have been introduced, exercise material can help children fix the visual-auditory relationship involved in the single-vowel-in-medial-position generalization. To use the following material, children should be told that the words in each line are exactly the same except for the vowel letter-sound.

1. "Listen for the difference (vowel sound) in each word."

2. "If the word is underlined, it is a nonsense word you haven't met—but you still can pronounce it."

3. "Read across each line of words."

a	*e*	*i*	*o*	*u*
bag	beg	big	bog	bug
→	→	→	→	
lad	led	lid	lod	lud
pat	pet	pit	pot	pud
dask	desk	disk	dosk	dusk
jag	jeg	jig	jog	jug
ham	hem	him	hom	hum
fan	fen	fin	fon	fun
Nat	net	nit	not	nut

lack	leck	lick	lock	luck
sap	sep	sip	sop	sup

● BLEND AND SAY

Teacher: "Each word has a blank space. A vowel letter is shown above each blank space. Think of the sound of the vowel letter and say each word."

a	*e*	*i*	*o*	*u*
b__t	b__d	h__t	h__p	f__n
a	*e*	*i*	*o*	*u*
c__n	j__t	p__g	l__g	b__s
e	*u*	*o*	*i*	*a*
m__n	g__m	c__t	s__x	f__t
i	*o*	*a*	*u*	*e*
d__g	m__p	r__t	f__n	l__g

● CHANGE THE VOWEL

Teacher: "Change the vowel and make a naming word for something living using the vowels *a, e, i, o,* or *u.*"

Examples:
cot—cat
pep—pup

dig	d__g	big	b__g
dock	d__ck	limb	l__mb
pit	p__t	crib	cr__b
cot	c__t	bell	b__ll
fix	f__x	peg	p__g

● WRITE AND SAY

This material can be presented in many different ways, including the chalkboard and duplicated exercises.
Teacher: "Put the vowel *a* in each of the following blank spaces. Then pronounce the word."

t__p	b__d
n__p	d__d
l__p	h__d
m__p	m__d
c__p	s__d

Teacher: "Put the vowel *e* in each of the following blank spaces. Then pronounce the word."

m__n	l__t
p__n	n__t
d__n	p__t
h__n	j__t
t__n	b__t

Teacher: "Put the vowel *i* in each of the following blank spaces. Pronounce the word."

p__n	h__t
t__n	b__t
b__n	s__t
f__n	f__t
s__n	p__t

Teacher: "Put the vowel *u* in each of the following blank spaces. Pronounce the word."

r__g	r__n
j__g	s__n
h__g	f__n
t__g	g__n
d__g	b__n

Teacher: "Add a vowel to make a word. Only one vowel fits in each word."

Examples:

w__b   (e)   *a, e, i, o, u*
f__sh (i)

1. y__s	**7.** gl__d	**13.** k__ss
2. v__m	**8.** r__ch	**14.** pl__n
3. sw__n	**9.** y__t	**15.** b__s
4. cl__b	**10.** s__ch	**16.** m__lk
5. r__ch	**11.** d__st	**17.** s__nt
6. k__g	**12.** d__t	**18.** n__st

Combining Teaching of Initial and Medial Vowel Sounds

Some teachers prefer to teach the short sound of initial and medial vowels simultaneously. The procedure can be much the same as for the medial-vowel situation; however, the generalization that emerges will be stated differently. To illustrate this concept, place a number of stimulus words on the board.

a	*a*
am	ham
ask	task
at	bat
and	sand
as	gas
act	fact
an	pan

Words in the first column contain one initial vowel, and the short sound is heard. Words in the second column contain one medial vowel, and the short sound is heard. As children see and hear the letter-sound relationship, the generalization will emerge: "When the only vowel in a word does not come at the end of the word it usually has its short sound."

LONG VOWEL (GLIDED) LETTER-SOUNDS

In teaching the long vowel letter-sounds, keep in mind that children differentiate these sounds when they process or use oral language. In the reading process, teaching the long vowel letter-sounds focuses primarily on having children recognize several visual patterns and associate these with the sounds they characteristically represent.

Using Visual Patterns as Cues to Sounding

Despite the large number of exceptions to any generalizations advanced to cover vowel letter-sounds, certain visual cues must be heeded. We will look at the following major patterns:

Two adjacent vowels (particularly m*ee*t, s*ea*t, c*oa*t, s*ai*l)

Medial vowel and final *e* (r*o*p*e*, c*a*p*e*, c*u*t*e*, t*i*r*e*)

Single vowel that concludes a word (g*o*, m*e*)

How *y* functions at the end of words (m*y*, ma*y*)

Two adjacent vowels are covered by the generalization "When two vowels come together, the first one usually has its long sound and the second is not sounded."

Data from studies of a large sample of words met in elementary reading materials indicate that this generalization actually applies to less than half the words that meet the two-vowel criterion; however, the generalization held fairly consistently for the *ee*, *oa*, *ai*, and *ea* patterns. Studies revealed the percentage of instances in which the two-vowel rule applies: *ee*, 98%; *oa*, 97%; *ai*, 64%; *ea*, 66%; and all two-vowel situations combined, 48% (Oaks, 1952; Clymer, 1963).

In the following examples, teaching does not start with a statement of generalizations but with material that emphasizes the visual patterns *oa*, *ee*, *ai*, *ea*. The patterns are linked to the sound heard in words and permit the children to discover the relationship and arrive at the generalization.

1. Place a column of *oa* words on the board: *boat, coat, load, road,* and *soak.*

2. Pronounce each word, emphasizing the long ō sound.

3. Have children note the visual pattern of the two vowels.

4. Point out that in each word you hear the long sound of the first vowel and the second vowel is not sounded. This may be illustrated, as in the right-hand column.

boat	bōa̸t
coat	cōa̸t
load	lōa̸d
road	rōa̸d
soak	sōa̸k

A similar procedure can be followed to introduce the patterns *ai, ea,* and *ee:*

ai		*ea*		*ee*	
chain	chāi̸n	beat	bēa̸t	feed	fēe̸d
mail	māi̸l	dream	drēa̸m	seed	sēe̸d
wait	wāi̸t	leaf	lēa̸f	keep	kēe̸p
rain	rāi̸n	teach	tēa̸ch	queen	quēe̸n
paid	pāi̸d	seat	sēa̸t	steel	stēe̸l

Teaching Short and Long Sounds Together

Some teachers prefer to present short and long sounds simultaneously. This procedure permits children to see both patterns (single and double vowel letters) and to contrast the sounds in familiar words. Material can be presented in two- or three-step fashion.

Teacher: "Today we want to practice hearing the difference between two sounds of the vowel letter *a.* In the first column, each word has one vowel letter. In the second column, each word has two vowels together."

ran	rain
pad	paid
bat	bait
lad	laid
pal	pail
mad	maid
pan	pain

1. Pronounce the words in the first column; then have the children read these words.

2. Have children note the following:

    a. Each word has one vowel.

    b. The vowel is in the middle of the word.

    c. The short sound (ă) of the vowel is heard.

3. Repeat the procedure for the words in the second column, having children note the following:

a. Each word contains the vowel pattern *ai*.

b. They say and hear the letter *a* (ā).

c. They do not sound or hear the second vowel letter.

The three-step approach permits children to see the process of adding a second vowel. This produces a new word containing two vowels that represent the long vowel sound heard.

One Vowel	Add i	New Word	
ă	↓	ā	
ran	ra*i*n	rā*i*n	(second vowel
pad	pa d	pāid	not sounded)
bat	ba t	bāit	
lad	la d	lāid	
pal	pa l	pāil	
mad	ma d	māid	
pan	pa n	pāin	

These words can be used to teach the other two-vowel patterns, *ee, ea,* and *oa:*

ă	ēė	ĕ	ēą	ŏ	ōą
bet	beet	set	seat	cot	coat
met	meet	men	mean	got	goat
fed	feed	bet	beat	rod	road
step	steep	bed	bead	Tod	toad
pep	peep	met	meat	cost	coast

● **USING CONTEXT**

Teacher: "Read the clue. Complete the word that fits the clue. Use one of the vowel patterns *a—e, i—e,* or *o—e* to spell the word."

Example:

Clue

Opening in fence   g__t__   (*a—e* for *gate*)

A pretty flower   r__s__   (*o—e* for *rose*)

Clue		Clue	
ten cents	d__m__	sticky stuff	p__st__
a brief letter	n__t__	a two-wheeler	b__k__
a number	n__n__	a body of water	l__k__

glass in window   p__n__   a funny story   j__k__

where there's fire   sm__k__   go fly a   k__t__

Teacher: "Use one of the vowel patterns *ai, ee,* or *ea* to spell the word."

Clue		Clue	
used for thinking	br_____n	a lady ruler	qu_____n
falls from clouds	r_____n	when it hurts	p_____n
a vegetable	b_____t	path in woods	tr_____l
to cure the sick	h_____l	along the ocean	b_____ch
not very strong	w_____k	back of foot	h_____l

Teacher: "The two words *not* and *note* fit in the two blanks in each sentence. Study each sentence and fill in the blanks."

1. He did _____ see the _____.

2. The _____ was _____ seen.

3. Why did he _____ see the _____?

4. Was the _____ seen or _____?

5. No, the _____ was _____ seen.

Teacher: "One of the words *met* or *meet* will fit in each blank space. Complete each sentence."

Examples:

Did you ____meet____ the new teacher?

Yes, we ____met____ yesterday.

1. _____ me at the ball game.

2. They _____ last year at camp.

3. The boys _____ at the track _____.

4. She will _____ us at four o'clock.

5. He said, "_____ me where we _____ last time."

Teacher: "All these sentences contain two blank spaces. Each word following a sentence will fit in one blank space. You decide which one."

Example:

When the ____rain____ started, he ____ran____ home.   ran
rain

1. They _____ at the _____ market.   met
meat

2. Some of the _____ were _____.   mean
men

3. Do not _____ it where you _____ it before.   hid
hide

4. The doctor said, "You _____ walk with a _____." cane
can

5. She _____ some of the people _____. mad
made

● FUN WITH LANGUAGE

Teacher: "In each sentence, three words need a pair of vowels. Write *ee, ea,* or *oa* in each blank space."

1. T_____ch children to k_____p off the r_____d.

2. You don't f_____d m_____t to a g_____t.

3. We n_____d a r_____l rain to s_____k the ground.

4. It's hard to k_____p a c_____l mine cl_____n.

5. We n_____d some m_____t and a l_____f of bread.

6. I f_____l like having r_____st beef and pie with my m_____l.

7. It was m_____n to k_____p the g_____t tied up.

Teacher: "Each of the following sentences contains two words with missing vowels. The clue tells you which vowel patterns will fit. Read the sentence to learn where they fit."

Set 1
Clues to Use: ee, oa, *and* ea

1. M_____t me at the m_____t market.

2. He sat near the r_____d to r_____d his book.

3. The doctor said, "This will h_____l your injured h_____l.

4. She took a last p_____k at the high mountain p_____k.

Set 2
Clues to Use: ea, ai, *and* oa

1. If we s_____l to the island we may see the s_____l.

2. The guide said, "Put the b_____t in the b_____t."

3. The g_____t walked with a funny g_____t.

4. Is the r_____l made of r_____l walnut wood?

Two Vowels, One of Which Is Final *e*

The generalization for this C-V-C-V pattern is "In words with two vowels, the second being final *e*, the first vowel usually has its long sound and the final *e* is not sounded." Clymer (1963) found that the pronunciation of 60% of the final-e words in his sample were governed by this generalization. Again, material can be presented so that children see the pattern, hear the long vowel sound, and arrive at the generalization.

1. Write on the board words that have a single vowel in medial position. Choose words to which a final *e* may be added to form a new word.

2. In an adjacent column, print these final-e words.

3. Have children pronounce these pairs of words, listening to the difference in the vowel sounds.

Stress the visual pattern vowel + e, and guide children in verbalizing the generalization: "In words with two vowels, the second being final e, the final e is not sounded and the first vowel usually has its long sound." You can use diacritical marks as shown in column C.

A	B	C
hat	hate	hāt̸e
hid	hide	hīd̸e
past	paste	pāst̸e
pal	pale	pāl̸e
cut	cute	cūt̸e
plan	plane	plān̸e
rat	rate	rāt̸e
pin	pine	pīn̸e
strip	stripe	strīp̸e
rid	ride	rīd̸e

● **FUN WITH LANGUAGE**

Teacher: "In each sentence, two words need a vowel. The same vowel letter fits in both blanks. One word will have its short sound; the other will have the long sound. Write in the vowel that makes sense."

1. John said, "I would h＿te to lose my new h＿t."

2. Do n＿t forget to leave a n＿te.

3. I h＿pe the rabbit will not h＿p on the flowers.

4. His friend P＿te has a p＿t turtle.

5. A r＿t can run at a very fast r＿te.

6. Their job was to c＿t out some c＿te cartoons.

7. Under the p＿ne tree, he found a pretty p＿n.

8. If you h＿d there once, don't h＿de there again.

Teacher: "Every word with a blank space ends with a silent e. Each blank space needs a vowel. This vowel will have its long vowel sound. Complete all of the words so that each sentence makes sense."

1. D__ve, M__ke, and K__te m__de plans for a picnic.

2. M__ke will b__ke a c__ke.

3. K__te will t__ke a l__me-and-lemon drink.

4. D__ve will t__ke a pl__te of r__pe fruit.

5. Later, D__ve and M__ke met K__te at the l__ke.

6. She r__de her b__ke; she l__kes to r__de it.

7. They will w__de in the l__ke, then t__ke a h__ke.

Single Final Vowels

When the only vowel in a word comes at the end of the word, it usually has its long sound. There probably are enough high-frequency words covered by this generalization to justify calling it to children's attention.

1. Place on the board words that contain one vowel in final position.

2. Have the children pronounce each word, noting the vowel at the end of the word and the sound it represents.

3. Invite children to supply a generalization covering these words (one final vowel has the long sound).

Notable exceptions to this generalization include *do, to, who,* and *two.* In words that end with *y* and that contain no other vowel, the *y* functions as a vowel. In these words the *y* is sounded as long ī (*my, by, try, fly, cry, dry, sky, shy*).

***At the end of words,* ay *has the sound of long* ā.** Children have learned that *y* functions as a vowel when it ends a word that has no other vowel letter. Here they learn that *y* following the vowel *a* fits a generalization learned previously: "When two vowels come together, the first usually has its long sound."

1. Place a few stimulus words on the board.

2. Lead the children in pronouncing these words.

3. Focus attention on the visual pattern *ay* and on the resulting sound of long ā.

4. Other words that fit this pattern: *play, hay, ray, pray, sway, jay, stray, gray, away,* and *tray.*

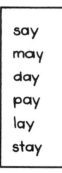

say
may
day
pay
lay
stay

Sound of y at the end of longer words. When *y* concludes a word of two or more syllables, it has the long sound of *e* heard in hob*by*, wind*y*, fog*gy*, luck*y*, jol*ly*, fun*ny*, hap*py*, mer*ry*, nois*y*, and rust*y*. Other words to use in teaching exercises are *badly, angry, plenty, honestly, closely, beauty, mainly, guilty, history, lively, nasty, January, partly, ready, seventy, rocky, penny, muddy, simply, sorry, jelly, nearly, costly,* and *sleepy.*

EXCEPTIONS TO VOWEL RULES PREVIOUSLY TAUGHT

There is no vowel rule or generalization that will apply in all situations. When exceptions to a given rule occur, they may be taught as sight words, or a new rule can be devised to cover the exception. It has been suggested that children not be burdened with rules that have limited applications. Different teachers will, of course, arrive at different conclusions as to which generalizations should be included in phonics instruction. Some exceptions to a given rule occur with such frequency as to merit calling children's attention to the exceptions.

For instance, one of the most useful phonic generalizations we have discussed states: "One vowel in medial position usually has its short sound." There are several series of words that meet the criterion of one vowel in medial position but in which the vowel has its long sound. For example, the vowel *o* followed by *ld* or *lt* usually has the long sound: *bold, mold, gold, sold, hold, told, fold, cold, colt, bolt, volt,* and *jolt.* Also, the vowel *i* followed by *nd, gh,* or *ld* frequently has the long sound: *find, blind, behind, mind, kind, light, fight, sight, right, wild, mild,* and *child.*

Two Adjacent Vowels

The generalization covering two adjacent vowels ("The first usually has its long sound; the second is not sounded.") has some exceptions in the patterns *oa, ai, ee,* and *ea.* While children are learning the words that follow the rule, they should also understand that exceptions will occur, such as *been, again, against, aisle, said, bread, break, head, dead, heart, steak,* and *broad.* There are many more exceptions found among other two-vowel patterns, including the following:

ei	ou	ie	au	ui, -ue, -ua
their	could	chief	caught	build
weigh	enough	field	laugh	guide
eight	rough	friend	fault	quiet
neighbor	should	piece	haunt	guess
vein	would	quiet	taught	guest
freight	touch	view	daughter	guard
rein	double	believe	haul	usual

Medial Vowel Plus Final *e*

Since a number of frequently met words, particularly *o* + *e* words, do not follow the generalization that one vowel in medial position usually has its short sound, some teachers prefer to deal with this fact rather than ignore it. Teachers might point out several exceptions, noting that applying the generalization will not help in solving the words *come, done, none, move, have, were, there, one, some, gone, love, glove, give, sense, where,* and *lose.*

VOWEL SOUNDS AFFECTED BY *R*

A vowel (or vowels) followed by the letter *r* results in a blended sound that is neither the short nor the long sound of the vowel. This phonic fact—as it relates to learning to read—is probably not extremely important; however, calling children's attention to this role of the letter *r* is a justifiable procedure. Since children use and understand hundreds of words that include a vowel followed by *r*, this is not a particularly difficult fact to teach. More important, children will have mastered several such words as sight words, and these can serve as examples when the generalization is introduced. Following are some of the more common vowel -*r* words for use in board work or seatwork exercises:

-ar		-er	-or
car	yard	her	for
farm	park	person	corn
march	card	term	storm
part	far	serve	horn
star	smart	ever	short
dark	arm	certain	north
hard	bark	berth	horse
barn	tar	herd	corner
start	spark	under	form

The spelling *ir* is usually pronounced *ûr* (bird = bûrd), except when followed by a final *e* (fire): *bird, dirt, firm, third, fir, thirst, girl, first, sir, shirt, birth,* and *stir.*

a FOLLOWED BY *L, LL, W,* AND *U*

The letter *a* has the sound ô (*aw*) when it is followed by *l, ll, w,* or *u;* for example:

talk	all	wall	saw	claw	haul
walk	tall	fall	draw	straw	because
salt	small	call	lawn	drawn	fault
halt	hall	ball	drawn	jaw	Paul

THE *OO* SOUNDS

Explaining the sounds of *oo* is much more complicated than actually learning to arrive at the correct pronunciation of the frequently used words that contain this letter combination. Most words containing *oo* are pronounced in one of two ways:

With the sound heard in *boo* and *boot*

With the sound heard in *book* and *foot*

Native speakers of English do not confuse these sounds while speaking or listening. When reading for meaning, children will not confuse the medial sounds heard in the two words used in each of these sentences:

The boot is larger than the foot.

The food is very good.

Beginning readers may not consciously note that the sounds are different because they never substitute one for the other. Practice in hearing differences can be provided by having children tell which of the following pairs of words rhyme:

cool—pool	food—good	soon—moon
boot—foot	book—look	look—hook
hoot—foot	wood—good	boot—hoot

The markings o͞o and ŏŏ may help children note the differences between these sounds, as in these sentences:

The bo͞ot is larger than the fŏŏt.

The mo͞ose drank from the co͞ol po͞ol.

He tŏŏk a lŏŏk at the brŏŏk.

In the final analysis, it is the context that helps children arrive at the correct pronunciation. For convenience in creating board or seatwork exercises, here are some o͞o and ŏŏ words:

o͞o				ŏŏ	
bo͞o	so͞on	mo͞on	bo͞ost	bŏŏk	fŏŏt
co͞ol	to͞ol	bro͞om	lo͞op	gŏŏd	tŏŏk

fo͞od	bo͞ot	po͞ol	ho͞ot		sto͝od	lo͝ok
ro͞om	bo͞on	lo͞ose	mo͞ose		sho͝ok	cro͝ok
to͞oth	zo͞o	ro͞ot	pro͞of		wo͝od	ho͝ok

A few *oo* words are neither o͞o or o͝o, such as *blood* (blŭd), *door* (dōr), *flood* (flŭd), and *floor* (flōr). These should be taught as sight words.

DIPHTHONGS

A diphthong is two adjacent vowels, each of which contributes to the sound heard. The diphthongs discussed here are *ou*, *oi*, and *oy*. In pronouncing diphthongs, the two vowel sounds are blended, as in *house, oil,* and *boy.*

1. The diphthongs *oi* and *oy* have the same sound (boy = bo*i*; boil = bo*i*l).
2. Sometimes *ow* represents the diphthong sound of *ou*.

Diphthong Sounds

1. Place several words on the board that illustrate the diphthong sound *oy* (column A).

2. In column B, change the spelling to *oi,* and in column C, add a final consonant to form a known word.

A		*B*		*C*
boy	→	boi	→	boil
toy	→	toi	→	toil
joy	→	joi	→	join
coy	→	coi	→	coin

3. Pronounce the words across each line, emphasizing that the *oy* and *oi* spellings represent the same sounds.

4. Point out that each vowel contributes to the sound heard.

5. Have children note that these vowel patterns do not follow the generalization that the first vowel has its long sound, and the second is not sounded.

Teaching that *ou* and *ow* represent the same sound may be done as follows:

1. Have children pronounce these pairs of words, noting that *ou* and *ow* represent the same sound.

owl	foul
crowd	cloud
fowl	ground

2. Place other *ou* and *ow* stimulus words on the board. In pronouncing the words in columns A and B, help children note that the letters *ou* and *ow* represent the same sound.

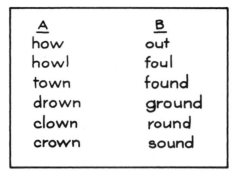

Words to use in board or seatwork drill include the following:

cow	owl	mouse	mouth	boil	boy
how	gown	sound	proud	coin	toy
brown	howl	loud	shout	toil	oyster
tower	brow	couch	found	joint	joy
crown	town	south	count	soil	Troy
powder	fowl	ground	bound	moist	employ

ow as the Long Sound of *o*

In a number of English words, the *ow* combination has the sound of ō. You can use the following steps to teach the sound.

1. The letter combination *ow* has two sounds: the diphthong sound heard in *plow* and the ō heard in *snow*.

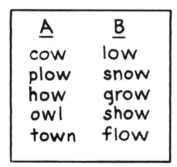

2. Pronounce the words in column A, with the children listening to the sound of *ow*.

3. Pronounce pairs of words (cow, low) with the children listening to contrasting sounds.

4. Have the children pronounce the words.

5. Point out that as words are read in context, the proper sound becomes obvious because the children know these words.

HOMONYMS

Homonyms are words that have the same pronunciation but different spellings and meanings. These words involve both structural and phonic analysis skills. Some homonyms follow one of the generalizations we have already introduced; many do not. For example, the rule "When two vowels occur together, the first is long, and the second is not sounded." applies to both words in the following pairs: *meet, meat; see, sea;* and *week, weak.*

Sometimes the rule applies to one word in a pair, and the final -e rule applies to the other word: *road, rode; sail, sale;* and *pain, pane.*

Some pairs involve unsounded consonants: *rap, wrap; new, knew;* and *our, hour.*

Other examples of phonic irregularities are *wait, weight; wood, would; ate, eight;* and *piece, peace.* The following exercises may be used or adapted to help children recognize homonyms that have irregular spellings.

● WORKING WITH HOMONYMS

1. Recognizing Homonyms
Directions: Explain the concept of homonyms: words that are pronounced the same but have different spellings and meanings. Have children pronounce the pairs of words at the left and answer the questions by writing *yes* or *no.*

	Same Spelling?	Same Sound?
there—their	_____	_____
ate—eight	_____	_____
two—to	_____	_____
would—wood	_____	_____
one—won	_____	_____
I—eye	_____	_____
some—sum	_____	_____
by—buy	_____	_____
our—hour	_____	_____
do—due	_____	_____

2. Matching Homonyms
Directions: Draw a line from the word in column A to the word in column B that is pronounced the same.

A	B		A	B
won	no		knot	blew
know	sew		blue	maid
so	one		made	not

pole	some		son	I
hour	eight		eye	sea
ate	our		pear	sun
sum	poll		see	pare

3. Match and Write Homonyms

Directions: Explain that each word in the clue box is pronounced like one of the words below the box. Children are to write the correct word on each blank space.

Clue Box							
eight	one	weigh	sew	some	would	wait	hole

so   _____   ate   _____

won   _____   sum   _____

way   _____   wood   _____

whole _____   weight _____

These are some common homonyms to use in board or seatwork exercises:

beat—beet	maid—made	pair—pare
know—no	I—eye	mail—male
hear—here	hair—hare	steel—steal
there—their	by—buy	waist—waste
sun—son	fair—fare	one—won
whole—hole	dear—deer	some—sum
oh—owe	not—knot	tail—tale

● USING CONTEXT

Teacher: "Two words follow each clue. These are homonyms: words pronounced the same but spelled differently. Read the clue and write the correct word in the blank space."

Example:

big price cut	_____ sale _____	sail	sale
Clue			
1. the ears do it	_____	here	hear
2. part of a window	_____	pain	pane
3. seven days in a	_____	week	weak
4. the eyes do it	_____	sea	see
5. an odd-shaped fruit	_____	pair	pear

6. fuel for a fireplace _____ wood would

7. a vegetable _____ beat beet

8. top of a mountain _____ peek peak

9. back part of the foot _____ heal heel

10. cars move on it _____ rode road

Teacher: "One of the words *weak* or *week* will fit in each blank space. Study each sentence and fill in the blanks."

Example:

There are seven days in a _____. (week)

He felt very _____ after the fever. (weak)

1. John was sick last _____.

2. He feels _____ this _____.

3. John has felt _____ since last _____.

4. Next _____, John will not be _____.

5. How did John feel last _____?

Teacher: "Each sentence has an underlined word and a blank space. In the blank space, write a homonym for the underlined word."

Examples:

We can be at our house in an _____. (hour)

Who knew about the _____ plans? (new)

1. The team won only _____ game.

2. Eight of the boys _____ all of the chicken.

3. _____ house is over there.

4. Would you please bring in some _____.

5. You can _____ the ocean if you come over here.

Teacher: "Each of these sentences has two missing words. The words *our* and *hour* will fit in each sentence. Where does each word fit?"

Example:

There was a one _____ meeting at _____ house.

Teacher: "Using the context of the sentence you would write: There was a one *hour* meeting at *our* house."

1. _____ game will start in one _____.

2. In about an _____ _____ game will start.

3. Will it take an _____ to play _____ game?

4. We can play _____ game in less than an _____.

Teacher: "The words *mail* and *male* are homonyms. Homonyms are words that are pronounced the same, but have different meanings. Each of these sentences has two missing words. The words *mail* and *male* will fit in each sentence. Where does each word fit?"

Example:

A _____ or a female may bring the _____.

Teacher: "Note that the context helps you get it right.
A *male* or a female may bring the *mail*."

1. When a _____ delivers the _____ he is called a mailman.

2. A _____ delivering the _____ is not a "maleman."

3. _____ can be delivered by a _____ or a female.

4. Who is the _____ delivering the _____ today?

5. That _____ delivering the _____ is Charlie.

THE SCHWA SOUND

In a large number of words of more than one syllable, there is a diminished stress on one of the syllables. The sound of the vowel in these unstressed syllables undergoes a slight change, referred to as a *softening* of the vowel sound. This softened vowel sound is called the *schwa sound,* and it is represented by the symbol ə.

All of the vowels are represented by the schwa sound, as illustrated by each of the italicized vowels in these words:

bedlam	=	bed'ləm
beaten	=	bē'tən
beautiful	=	bū'tə fəl
beckon	=	bek'ən

In other words, if vowels were interchanged in unstressed syllables, the spellings would change but the sound heard would remain the same for the different vowels. For instance, read both of these sentences without stressing the second syllable in any word:

> **A.** Button, button, who has the button?
> **B.** Buttun, buttan, who has the butten?

If, in reading sentence B, you give each second syllable the same stress as it was given in the word directly above it, the sounds remain constant. Thus, teaching the schwa sound in the initial stages of reading would have little impact on one's ability to sound out words. Once the child begins to use a dictionary that utilizes the schwa symbol, ə, however, these points should be explained.

SIGHT-WORD LIST

Table 6–1 is a list of words, most of which are met in primary reading, that illustrates irregular spellings. From the standpoint of spoken language, all words are phonetic; however, the spellings (visual patterns) of these words are such that the more common phonic generalizations learned in beginning reading will not apply.

TABLE 6–1 Sight-word List: Words with Irregular Spellings Resulting in Confusion Between Letters Seen and Sounds Heard

above	could	ghost	love	quiet	together
across	couple	give			ton
again	cousin	gives	machine	ranger	tongue
against	cruel	gloves	many	ready	too
aisle	curve	gone	measure	really	touch
already		great	might	right	two
another	dead	guard	mild	rough	
answer	deaf	guess	million		use
anxious	debt	guest	mind	said	usual
any	desire	guide	minute	says	
	do		mischief	school	vein
bear	does	have	mother	science	very
beautiful	done	head	move	scissors	view
beauty	don't	heart	Mr.	sew	
because	double	heaven	Mrs.	shoe	was
been	doubt	heavy		should	wash
behind	dove	here	neighbor	sign	weather
believe	dozen	high	neither	snow	weight
bind			night	soften	were
both	early	idea	none	soldier	what
bough	earn	Indian		some	where
bread	eight	instead	ocean	someone	who
break	enough	isle	of	something	whom
bright	eye		office	sometime	whose
brought	eyes	key	often	son	wild
build		kind	oh	soul	wind
built	father	knee	once	special	wolf
bury	fence	knew	one	spread	woman
busy	field	knife	onion	square	women
buy	fight	know	only	steak	won
	find		other	straight	would
calf	folks	language	ought	sure	wrong
captain	four	laugh		sword	
caught	freight	laughed	patient		you
chief	friend	leather	piece	their	young
child	front	library	pretty	there	your
clothes		light	pull	they	
colt	garage	lion	purpose	though	
coming	get	live	push	thought	
cough	getting	lived	put	to	

SUMMARY

There is considerable variability in the sounds of vowels and vowel combinations in English. This increases the difficulty of teaching or learning vowel sounds. The sequence in which vowel sounds are taught—that is, whether to teach long or short sounds first or which vowels to teach first—is probably not a significant issue. The teaching procedures in this chapter are meant to be illustrative rather than prescriptive.

Some generalizations covering vowel situations include the following:

- A single vowel in medial position in a word or syllable usually has its short sound (man, bed, fit).
- When two vowels are side by side in a word, the first usually has its long sound and the second is not sounded.
- When a word has two vowels, the second being final e, the first usually has its long sound and the final e is not sounded.
- *Ay* at the end of a word has the long sound of ā (may, pay, play).
- When the only vowel in a word (or accented syllable) comes at the end of the word (or syllable), it usually has its long sound.
- When *y* concludes a word of two or more syllables, it has the long sound of ē heard in *lucky* and *badly*.
- *Y* functions as a vowel when it concludes a word or syllable that has no other vowel:

my, sky, dy • ing, hy • phen

- falls in the middle of a syllable that has no other vowel:

sym • bol, syn • o • nym, typ • ist

- A diphthong is two adjacent vowels, each of which contributes to the sound heard (house, oil, boy).
- The combination *ow* is sometimes pronounced as ō (snow, show); the context provides the major clue to pronunciation.

7

STRUCTURAL
ANALYSIS SKILLS

Learning to read is a long-term, developmental process, and teaching a total word-analysis skills program is also developmental in nature. Previous chapters have presented data on letter-sound relationships; this chapter continues to deal with letter-sound relationships, but we will also stress other important word-analysis skills that fit under the broad heading of structural analysis. To maintain normal growth in reading, children must learn to recognize and react to certain features of written language, including (a) inflectional endings: *-s, -ed, -ing, -ly,* and so on; (b) compound words; (c) plural forms; (d) prefixes and suffixes; (e) syllabication; (f) contractions; and (g) accent within words.

As we have noted, when children meet a printed word that they do not instantly recognize, they have several options: (a) to sound out the word, (b) to use context clues, or (c) to combine these two approaches.

Early in beginning reading, children add another option, that of recognizing a root word imbedded among affixes. English orthography utilizes a number of structural changes that occur again and again in thousands of words. In learning to read, one must develop expertise in recognizing prefixes, suffixes, and inflectional endings.

To successfully master the structural variations that occur in English orthography, children must come to the reading task with certain skills and abilities. In essence, they must apply or transfer something they already know about letter-sounds and word forms to new situations. For example, assume that a child can recognize the word *ask* but has not yet met *asks, asked,* or *asking.* His prior experience and his ability to respond to *ask* should help him in decoding the inflected forms.

While the child still has the option of sounding out these new words, he also can use the established response to the word *ask.* If one is reading for meaning, this root clue plus the contextual demands of the passage will unlock the inflected forms that are used constantly in the child's oral language.

Different readers, however, will require a differing number of experiences and varied amounts of instruction to acquire the necessary insights. For some children, a prefix and suffix added to a known word tends to obscure what is known. In such cases more trials are needed for transfer to take place. All children must have a certain amount of practice in recognizing the visual patterns of words that result from the addition of affixes.

One factor that aids both the learner and the teacher is that a great majority of affixes represent the same sound(s) in thousands of different words. Thus, the major objective in working with structural changes in words is to teach children to instantly recognize these visual patterns in written English.

INFLECTIONAL ENDINGS

The word endings -s and -ed represent variations in letter-sound relationships that probably have little impact on learning to read. The fact that final s represents the sound of s in asks and z in dogs is not a cause of confusion to beginners. Nor is the fact that -ed in added, asked, and played is pronounced as ed, t, and d, respectively. The rules that govern these differences are complicated and are much more important to linguists than to native speakers of English whose objective is to learn to read English. Children have never heard, said, or read "The man work-ed hard." or "Where are my glove-s?"

Nonetheless, children will likely need some practice in visual recognition of inflected word forms because of the structural differences between these and known root words.

Adding *-s, -ed,* and *-ing* to Words

1. In the spaces provided, write the word on the left adding -s, -ed, and -ing.

2. Pronounce each word.

Word	-s	-ed	-ing
walk	_____	_____	_____
show	_____	_____	_____
look	_____	_____	_____
ask	_____	_____	_____
call	_____	_____	_____
answer	_____	_____	_____
load	_____	_____	_____
paint	_____	_____	_____

Adding *-er, -est,* and *-ly* to Words

1. Make new words by adding the endings -er, -est, and -ly to the root word on the left.

2. Pronounce each word.

3. How do these endings change the meaning of words?

Word	-er	-est	-ly
slow	_____	_____	_____
light	_____	_____	_____
warm	_____	_____	_____
soft	_____	_____	_____
bright	_____	_____	_____
calm	_____	_____	_____

Words ending with e. Drop the final *e* before adding a suffix beginning with a vowel.

Word	+ed	+ing	+er	+est	+ous
bake	baked	baking	baker		
trade	traded	trading	trader		
pale	paled		paler	palest	
fame	famed				famous
late			later	latest	

Adding Suffixes Following *y*

Change *y* to *i* before adding a suffix beginning with a vowel.

Word	Common Endings Beginning with a Vowel:			
	-ed	-er	-est	-ous
busy	busied	busier	busiest	
fury				furious
dry	dried	drier	driest	
muddy	muddied	muddier	muddiest	
happy		happier	happiest	
glory				glorious
carry	carried	carrier		

Exception: If the suffix begins with *i,* leave the *y: crying, drying, frying, flying, copying,* and *carrying.*

DOUBLING FINAL CONSONANTS

Explain to children the generalization, "Words that contain one vowel and end with a single consonant (beg, stop, fan) usually double that consonant before adding an ending beginning with a vowel," as in *begged, begging, beggar, stopped, stopping,* and *stopper.*

Teacher: "Look carefully at the words on lines 1, 2, and 3. Add the same endings to the other words."

Word	-ed	-ing	-er
1. log	logged	logging	logger
2. dim	dimmed	dimming	dimmer
3. stop	stopped	stopping	stopper
4. pop	_____	_____	_____
5. skip	_____	_____	_____
6. trot	_____	_____	_____
7. bat	_____	_____	_____
8. trap	_____	_____	_____
9. plan	_____	_____	_____
10. spot	_____	_____	_____

● USING CONTEXT

Teacher: "Each of the following sentences has a blank space. Complete each sentence using one word in the clue box that will make the sentence correct."

Clue Box
walks   walked   walk   walking

1. Can the baby _____?

2. Yes, the baby is _____ now.

3. She _____ yesterday.

4. She _____ every day.

5. She will _____ tomorrow.

Clue Box
slow   slowly   slows   slower   slowest

1. Who is the _____ runner on the team?

2. John is very _____.

3. He is _____ than Tom and Rob.

4. After he runs a while he _____ down.

5. But John is _____ improving.

Teacher: "In the following sentences, write the form of the word that makes the sentence correct."

fast   **1.** John is _____ than Bill, but Ted is the _____ runner on the team.

kind **2.** The mayor is a _____ old gentleman.

cold **3.** November is _____ than July.

short **4.** If they took the _____ trail they should arrive _____.

long **5.** What is the _____ word in the dictionary?

Teacher: "Each of these sentences is followed by three words. Two of these words will fit in the blank spaces. Read each sentence and fill in the blanks."

Example:

June is _____ but July is _____.   warm

June is _____warm_____ but July is _____warmer_____   warmer
                                                                        warmest

1. John _____, "Did anyone _____ for me?"   ask
                                                                        asking
                                                                        asked

2. She _____ yesterday and is also _____ today. paints
                                                                        painted
                                                                        painting

3. Speaking _____, John said, "Cotton is _____ than linen." softer
                                                                        softly
                                                                        softest

4. The car _____ at the _____ sign.   stop
                                                                        stopping
                                                                        stopped

5. It _____ yesterday and is _____ now.   rain
                                                                        rained
                                                                        raining

Teacher: "In each sentence there is a blank space with a root word below it. Add the proper ending to this word so that it will be correct in the sentence."

Example:

Mother is <u>bringing</u> cookies.

  1. The bird _____ its wings.
        (flap)

  2. We are _____ to leave tomorrow.
        (plan)

  3. We saw a _____ in the woods.
        (hunt)

  4. A man who cuts down trees in a forest is called a _____.
                    (log)

  5. One who traps animals is called a _____.
            (trap)

  6. The little dog was _____.
        (bark)

7. Who is the best _____ on the baseball team?
                        (hit)

8. John is the _____ _____ on the team.
                    (fast)   (run)

9. Two boys were _____ in the sand.
                        (dig)

10. The _____ it rained the _____ we got.
              (hard)   (wet)

COMPOUND WORDS

Mastery of compound words is a developmental process. Children meet a few compounds in first grade and an increasing number thereafter. They need to know that some words are formed by combining two or more words. In most instances children will be familiar with one or both words that make up a compound.

Recognition of compound words is achieved through every type of word-analysis skill: structural analysis, phonic analysis, and context examination. When teaching compound words, each of these aids should be employed. Learning sight words and structural phonic analysis actually go hand in hand. Keep these points in mind:

- Compound words are part of children's speaking and meaning vocabulary. When they meet compounds in reading, they will combine recognition and sounding techniques.
- The meaning of many compound words is derived from combining two words.
- The pronunciation of the compound word remains the same as for the two combining forms (except for accent or stress).
- Procedures for teaching compound words vary with the instructional level.

● BUILDING COMPOUND WORDS

1. Oral Exercise

Purpose: To provide practice in using compound words.

Directions: Explain to children the concept of compound words: combining two or more words to make a different word.

   Demonstrate on the chalkboard: some + thing = something
                                    some + one = someone
                                    some + time = sometime

Other words to use include *schoolhouse, barnyard, football, birdhouse, firefighter,* etc.

Teacher: "I'll say a word and you add a word to it to make another word."

   1. base _____ (ball)

   2. sail _____ (boat)

   3. door _____ (way, man, mat)

4. motor _____ (cycle, boat)

5. road _____ (way, side, block)

6. over _____ (head, board, shoe)

7. moon _____ (light, beam, glow)

8. air _____ (plane, port)

9. bath _____ (tub, house, room)

10. tooth _____ (brush, ache, paste)

2. Seeing Compound Words as Wholes and Breaking Them into Parts

Teacher: "Each of the words on the left is a compound word. Write the two words found in each compound word."

Example:

snowman _____snow_____ _____man_____

1. waterfall _____ _____

2. bluebird _____ _____

3. policeman _____ _____

4. notebook _____ _____

5. himself _____ _____

6. homework _____ _____

7. anyone _____ _____

8. seaside _____ _____

9. turnpike _____ _____

10. airplane _____ _____

3. More Compound Words

Teacher: "Combine one word from the clue box with each word below the box to form compound words."

Clue Box			
type	tooth	snap	after
any	grand	bed	light

_____ ache   _____ one

_____ noon   _____ writer

_____ father   _____ shot

_____ house   _____ room

To provide practice in recognizing and writing compound words, illustrate how the same word can be used in a number of compound words.

Teacher: "Using the word in the first column, write three compound words."
Example:

air	plane	craft	port
	airplane	*aircraft*	*airport*
1. book	case	keeper	worm
	_____	_____	_____
2. door	way	man	mat
	_____	_____	_____
3. candle	light	maker	stick
	_____	_____	_____
4. moon	glow	beam	light
	_____	_____	_____
5. down	town	wind	stream
	_____	_____	_____
6. shoe	lace	horn	maker
	_____	_____	_____

Teacher: "Each line contains one compound word. Underline the compound word and write it on the blank space at the end of the line."

1. children	dancing	hotdog	_____
2. someone	beaches	crawling	_____
3. alike	mousetrap	puzzle	_____
4. downpour	happily	permitted	_____
5. autumn	mistake	handbag	_____

4. Identifying Compound Words

Directions: Some of the following are compound words, and some are two words written together that do not make a word. Have the children underline the compound words.

beehive	ballback	ballpark
anyelse	everyone	everysome
roommate	roompost	signpost
aftermuch	afternoon	afterman
fireplace	photodog	overland
overleft	houseboat	housemake
nearby	overstill	lifeboat

5. Using Context

Directions: Have the children underline each compound word. Then have them draw a line between the two words in each compound (mail/box).

1. Everyone went to the football game that afternoon.

2. Josh is upstairs writing in his scrapbook with his ballpoint pen.

3. We ran halfway to the clubhouse without stopping.

4. Doug received a flashlight, a raincoat, and a sailboat for his birthday.

5. He read the newspaper headline, "Big fire at sawmill."

6. They saw the shipwreck from a hilltop near the lighthouse.

6. Sentence Completion

Directions: Develop a series of sentences in which a common compound will complete the sentence, then have children read the sentence and write the compound word. Material can be presented orally, or by means of the chalkboard, transparencies, or duplicated exercises. The first exercise is made easy by presenting the compound words in scrambled order above the sentences. In the second exercise, the children provide the words.

baseball	mailbox	bedroom
raincoat	football	seashore

A.

1. Letters are mailed in a _____.

2. The room we sleep in is called a _____.

3. A bat is used in the game of _____.

4. The girls gathered shells at the _____.

5. A _____ field has goalposts at each end of the field.

6. Mother said, "It's raining; be sure and wear your _____."

B.

1. A player can hit a home run in the game of _____.

2. The teacher wrote on the _____ with a piece of chalk.

3. The airplane landed at the _____.

4. The front window in a car is called the _____.

5. The mailman puts mail in our _____.

7. Combining Words to Make Compounds

Directions: Have children add the correct word in sentences 1 and 2, then combine those two words in sentence 3.

Example:

1. The opposite of work is _____. (play)
                                  1

2. In the spring we plant seeds in the _____. (ground)
                                            2

3. We go to the _____ at recess. (playground)
            1 & 2

1. Let's take our sleds and play in the _____.
1

2. The pitcher threw the _____ over the plate.
2

3. We like to have _____ fights in the winter.
1 & 2

1. The house we live in is called our _____.
1

2. The opposite of play is _____.
2

3. School work we do at home is called _____.
1 & 2

1. A mailman delivers the _____.
1

2. He carries the mail in a _____.
2

3. The mailman carries the mail in a _____.
1 & 2

Teacher: "Each sentence contains a blank space. Select a word from the clue box that will complete a compound word."

Examples:

Clue Box		
snap	house	grand

1. Mother read the letter from our _____ father.

2. The letter contained a _____ shot.

3. It showed our grandfather in front of a light _____.

Clue Box			
way	point	wreck	some
brush	house	teller	star

1. John lost his ball_____ pen.

2. The captain gave details about the ship_____.

3. The sign read, "Don't block the door_____."

4. Some of the golfers ate dinner at the club_____.

5. Susan found a_____fish on the beach.

6. Grandfather was a great story_____.

7. _____one will have to help the guide.

8. Clean the paint_____ when you finish painting.

WORKING WITH PLURALS

Forming plurals by adding *s, es,* or *ies* results in structural changes in word forms that can be puzzling to children in their early reading experience. Exercises can help children instantly recognize the plurals of common root words.

Adding *-s* to Form Plurals

1. Illustrate the singular-plural concept at the chalkboard using any words to which the letter *-s* is added to form a plural (book—books, hat—hats, chair—chairs). Teach the concept that *plural* means "more than one."

2. Write the plural of each word on the blank space.

cup	_____	game	_____
rat	_____	bag	_____
fan	_____	kitten	_____
boat	_____	comb	_____
desk	_____	nail	_____
rabbit	_____	table	_____
king	_____	ship	_____
crop	_____	sled	_____

3. Prepare materials similar to the illustrations.

4. Read the sentences with the children.

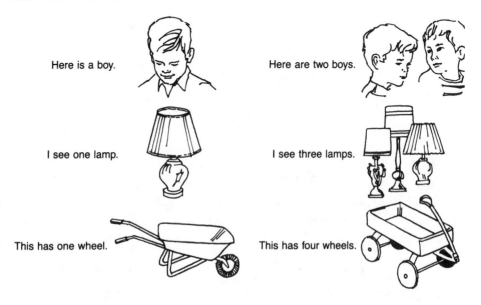

Here is a boy.

Here are two boys.

I see one lamp.

I see three lamps.

This has one wheel.

This has four wheels.

Plurals Formed by Adding -es

Teach the concept that words ending with *s, ss, ch, sh,* and *x* form plurals by the addition of *-es.* Use the chalkboard or duplicated handouts to present material similar to the following.

When do we add *-es* to show more than one?
When words end with

ss	ch	sh	x
dress	church	dish	box
dresses	*churches*	*dishes*	*boxes*

Teacher: "Write the plural for each word."

glass	_____	brush	_____
pass	_____	wish	_____
cross	_____	crash	_____
witch	_____	fox	_____
watch	_____	six	_____
inch	_____	tax	_____

Teacher: "Practice reading these words."

matches	sketches	speeches	benches	waxes
splashes	wishes	batches	ashes	fusses
beaches	kisses	gulches	hisses	birches
bosses	dashes	misses	lashes	gashes

Plurals of Words Ending with *y*

When a word ends with *y,* its plural is formed by changing the *y* to *i* and adding *-es.*

city—cit*ies*   lady—lad*ies*   fairy—fair*ies*

Teacher: "Write the plural for each of these words."

baby	_____	party	_____	cherry	_____
puppy	_____	body	_____	buddy	_____
army	_____	fly	_____	berry	_____

● RECOGNITION OF PLURALS

Teacher: "Each of the following words means that there is more than one. These plurals were formed by adding *-s, -es,* or (*y* =) *-ies.* Read these words as quickly as possible."

porches	foxes	cubs	lunches	watches	witches
girls	benches	guesses	coaches	inches	taxes

speeches	peaches	dresses	answers	matches	candies
funnies	factories	cookies	berries	pennies	armies
buses	glasses	frogs	boxes	brushes	dishes

Other Plural Forms

Some plurals involve vowel changes within the word: *foot—feet, man—men, goose—geese, mouse—mice, tooth—teeth,* and *woman—women.*

For words ending with *f,* change *f* to *v* and add *es:* wolf—wolves, shelf—shelves, calf—calves, loaf—loaves, thief—thieves, and *leaf—leaves.*

Some singular and plural forms have the same spelling: *deer—deer, sheep—sheep,* and *moose—moose.*

For words ending with *o* following a consonant, add *es:* potato—potatoes, echo—echoes, hero—heroes, and *zero—zeroes.*

● USING CONTEXT

Teacher: "The words in column A each mean that there is only one. If the word under *Clue* means that there is more than one, write the plural of the word in column A on the blank space."

Example:

goose	these	_____geese_____
A	*Clue*	
lady	one	_____
church	many	_____
city	some	_____
bench	a	_____
bird	a flock of	_____
potato	four	_____
house	this	_____
wolf	a pack of	_____
man	that	_____
sheep	several	_____

Teacher: "In each blank space, write the plural form of the underlined word in the sentence."

Examples:

The <u>woman</u> had been speaking to the _____. (women)

There were many new _____ in the <u>dress</u> shop. (dresses)

1. The board was a <u>foot</u> wide and ten _____ long.

2. Put this <u>dish</u> in with the clean _____.

3. Many _____ claim to be the "most beautiful <u>city</u>."

4. The young <u>wolf</u> watched the older _____ hunt.

5. This <u>watch</u> is more expensive than the other _____.

6. The <u>spy</u> story was written by two _____.

7. There were many _____ in the <u>bus</u> station.

8. He asked the <u>boy</u> where the other _____ were playing.

9. That <u>lady</u> is president of the _____ group.

10. Put all of the smaller _____ in the largest <u>box</u>.

Teacher: "In each blank space, write the plural of the italicized word."

1. There was one _pony_ in the pasture.

There were two _____ in the pasture.

2. The police captured a _spy._

The police captured three _____.

3. Each _lady_ bought a hat.

All the _____ bought hats.

4. One _fly_ flew away.

Both _____ flew away.

5. John lost one _penny._

John lost several _____.

PREFIXES AND SUFFIXES

As children progress in reading, they will meet many words that contain prefixes and suffixes. Teaching aimed at making each child an independent reader will have to deal with structural analysis, phonic analysis, and syllabication. In addition, the teaching of reading will have to focus on the changes in meaning that result when affixes are added to root words.

Many children develop the attitude that they will be unsuccessful in solving longer polysyllabic words, and they give up easily. Thus, their fears are self-fulfilling. One of the objectives of the following exercises is to provide hints that will help readers unlock such words. Children are led to see that English writing contains many prefabricated units (prefixes and suffixes). A number of clues are pointed out, namely that these affixes

Are spelled the same in thousands of different words and thus have the same visual pattern

Have the same pronunciation in different words

Consistently appear before or after a root word

Are usually syllables

The procedures and materials in example A focus on having children see and combine root words with prefixes and suffixes while pronouncing the words formed. Examples B and C stress syllabication.

A. Each line begins with a root word to which three prefixes are added. The children pronounce these words, noting the visual patterns resulting from the prefixes.

Root	+ pre	+ re	+ un
pack	prepack	repack	unpack
wind	prewind	rewind	unwind
paid	prepaid	repaid	unpaid

Root	+ dis	+ mis	+ re
place	displace	misplace	replace
use	disuse	misuse	reuse
count	discount	miscount	recount

B. The first word in each column is a root word; the second has a common prefix; the third, a common word ending.

Root	+ dis	+ ment
appoint	dis/appoint	dis/appoint/ment
agree	dis/agree	dis/agree/ment
place	dis/place	dis/place/ment

Root	+ re	+ able
clean	re/clean	re/clean/able
form	re/form	re/form/able
charge	re/charge	re/charge/able

Root	+ in	+ ness
complete	in/complete	in/complete/ness
direct	in/direct	in/direct/ness
visible	in/visible	in/visible/ness
human	in/human	in/human/ness

C. The first word in each column is a root word; a suffix has been added in the second; and another suffix in the third.

Root	+ less	+ ness
use	useless	uselessness
speech	speechless	speechlessness
sight	sightless	sightlessness

Root	+ ful	+ ness
watch	watchful	watchfulness
truth	truthful	truthfulness
play	playful	playfulness

D. This material stresses the structural (visual) changes resulting from adding affixes. It includes some inflected endings taught previously.
1. Read each line of words in unison with the class.
2. Have a volunteer read the same line of words.
3. Have similar exercises available for individual practice.

agree	agrees	disagree	disagreement	agreeable
fill	refill	filled	refilled	refilling
place	placed	replaced	replacement	places
honor	honorable	dishonor	dishonorable	honored
hope	hopeless	hopeful	hopefully	hoping

E. For practice in building new words by writing common endings, form a new word by writing the ending shown above each group of words.

ment				*ness*	
pay	_____	agree	_____	blind	_____	deaf	_____
state	_____	pave	_____	dry	_____	clever	_____
move	_____	treat	_____	close	_____	kind	_____
enjoy	_____	punish	_____	bold	_____	polite	_____
base	_____	excite	_____	calm	_____	like	_____

ful		*less*		*able*	
hope	_____	hope	_____	wash	_____
cheer	_____	cheer	_____	honor	_____
doubt	_____	doubt	_____	comfort	_____
grace	_____	cloud	_____	agree	_____
dread	_____	sleep	_____	change	_____

● USING CONTEXT

Teacher: "Note the underlined word in each clue. Add a prefix and suffix to that word so that the new word fits the clue."

Example:

to not deserve <u>trust</u>.   (un)trust(worthy)

Helpers: | dis-   un- | | -ful   -able   -ment   -ness |

1. you can't avoid it   _____avoid_____

2. a failure to agree   _____agree_____

3. can't depend on him   _____depend_____

4. not being happy is?   _____happi_____

5. does not tell the truth   _____truth_____

6. opposite of or lack of honor   _____honor_____

Teacher: "Note the underlined word in each clue. Add an ending to that word so that the new word fits the clue."

Example:

Some <u>doubt</u> that it will happen.   doubt(ful)

Helpers: | -able   -ful   -less   -ness   -or |

1. no change over the years   change_____

2. can depend on him   depend_____

3. always being idle   idle_____

4. has little or no use   use_____

5. results in pain   pain_____

6. shows grace in dancing   grace_____

7. his job is to act   act_____

To help children achieve mastery of root words plus affixes, use the following paragraphs for reading practice. Read one paragraph, then select a volunteer to read. Tell students, "As we read each paragraph, note the meaning of the underlined words."

The Governor said, "I doubt that the bridge will be built. Doubtless, many of you would like to see it built. However, it is quite doubtful that funds will be available." Informed observers agree that this is doubtlessly true.

Advertisers spend money on advertising because advertisements help to advertise what they have to sell.

A towel will absorb water. This towel is absorbing water. Now it has absorbed about all it can. It absorbs because it is made of absorbent material.

A mountain climber must care about safety. Mountain climbers who care will be careful, not careless. Carelessness in the face of danger does not lead to a carefree climb. When plans are thought out carefully, one is not likely to act carelessly.

For writing practice, tell students to write a paragraph using all (or as many as possible) of the words on each line.

beauty, beautiful, beautifully
joy, joyful, joyfully, joyous, joyless, joylessly
help, helpful, helpfulness, helpless, helplessness
war, prewar, postwar, prowar, antiwar, warlike

SYLLABICATION

A syllable is a vowel or a group of letters containing a vowel sound that together form a pronounceable unit. The ability to break words into syllables is an important word-analysis skill that cuts across both phonic and structural analysis. Syllabication is an aid in

Pronouncing words not instantly recognized as sight words

Arriving at the correct spelling of many words

Breaking words at the end of a line of writing

Two major clues to syllabication are prefixes and suffixes, and certain vowel-consonant behavior in written words. Thus, the ability to solve the pronunciations represented by many longer printed words is built on the recognition of both structural and phonetic features.

Much of the material regarding prefixes and suffixes can be used for teaching syllabication, as well as visual recognition of word parts. This chapter section continues to build recognition of prefixes and suffixes but also stresses how these function as syllables. With practice, syllabication tends to become an automatic process. To illustrate, there will be considerable agreement among adult readers when they pronounce the following nonsense words: *dismorative, unmurly, interlate,* and *motoption.* The syllabication patterns arrived at would probably be *dis·mor·a·tive, un·mur·ly, in·ter·late,* and *mo·top·tion.* In addition, there would probably be relatively high agreement as to which syllable was to receive the primary accent: *dis·mor'·a·tive, un·mur'·ly, in'·ter·late,* and *mo·top'·tion.*

The reader's pronunciation of these nonsense words probably did not involve calling to mind rules that might apply, yet the responses were undoubtedly conditioned by previous learning and experiences that relate to principles of syllabication. Despite numerous exceptions to some generalizations dealing with syllabication, other generalizations may be useful to students aspiring to become independent readers.

Generalizations Relating to Syllabication

1. There are as many syllables in a word as there are vowel sounds. Syllables are determined by the vowel sounds heard, not by the number of vowels seen.

	Vowels Seen		Vowels Heard		Vowels Seen		Vowels Heard
measure	(4)	mezh'er	(2)	moment	(2)	mō' ment	(2)
phonics	(2)	fon iks	(2)	cheese	(3)	chēz	(1)
write	(2)	rīt	(1)	which	(1)	hwich	(1)
release	(4)	rē lēs	(2)	precaution	(5)	prē kô shun	(3)
skill	(1)	skill	(1)	receive	(4)	rē sēv'	(2)

2. Syllables divide between double consonants or between two consonants.

hap·pen	can·non	sud·den	ves·sel	vol·ley	com·mand
bas·ket	tar·get	cin·der	har·bor	tim·ber	wig·wam
don·key	pic·nic	gar·den	lad·der	let·ter	sup·per

3. A single consonant between vowels usually goes with the second vowel.

fa mous	ho tel	di rect	ti ger	ce ment	pu pil
ea ger	wa ter	po lice	lo cate	va cant	spi der
be gin	fi nal	be fore	pi lot	li bel	sto ry
pa rade	e lect	re ceive	lo cal	sta tion	be hind

The previous two generalizations are often combined: Divide between two consonants and in front of one.

4. As a general rule, do not divide consonant digraphs (*ch, th,* etc.) and consonant blends.

tea*ch* er	wea*th* er	ma *chine*	se *cret*	a *gree*
bro*th* er	prea*ch* er	a*th* lete	coun *try*	cel e *brate*

5. The word endings *-ble, -cle, -dle, -gle, -kle, -ple, -tle,* and *-zle* form the final syllable.

mar ble	mus cle	han dle	sin gle	an kle	tem ple
ket tle	puz zle	no ble	pur ple	bat tle	bu gle

The following list of words can be used in building board or seatwork exercises. Instruct your students to practice these words so they can recognize and pronounce each one instantly. Point out how easy it is to learn to spell the words.

no ble	rat tle	sin gle	han dle	tem ple	an kle
mar ble	ket tle	wig gle	mid dle	ma ple	spar kle
sta ble	ti tle	jun gle	pad dle	ap ple	wrin kle
tum ble	bat tle	strug gle	bun dle	sam ple	sprin kle
trou ble	bot tle	gig gle	fid dle	pur ple	crin kle
fa ble	gen tle	bu gle	bri dle	stee ple	tin kle
dou ble	cat tle	ea gle	nee dle	sim ple	puz zle
rum ble	man tle	an gle	sad dle	un cle	fiz zle
peb ble	set tle	shin gle	kin dle	cir cle	muz zle
bub ble	lit tle	strag gle	pud dle	ve hi cle	daz zle

6. Usually, prefixes and suffixes form separate syllables.

re load ing	un fair	dis agree ment	pre heat ed
hope less	trans port ing	un like ly	ex cite ment

Affixes as Syllables

As we have noted, many prefixes and word endings constitute syllables that are highly consistent in regard to spelling and pronunciation. When children encounter difficulty in attacking and solving longer words, experiences should be provided that help them see the spelling and syllable patterns. The following lessons can help children recognize polysyllabic words that contain a prefix, suffix, or both.

● SEEING SYLLABLES IN LONGER WORDS

A. Read down each column.

lo	con	dis
lo co	con ver	dis a
lo co mo	con ver sa	dis a gree
lo co mo tive	con ver sa tion	dis a gree ment

B. Read down each column.

lo	con	dis
lo co	con ver	dis a
lo co mo	con ver sa	dis a gree
lo co mo tive	con ver sa tion	dis a gree ment
lo co mo	con ver sa	dis a gree
lo co	con ver	dis a
lo	con	dis
locomotive	*conversation*	*disagreement*

C. Read across each line as quickly as you can.

locomotive	lo	lo co	lo co mo	locomotive
conversation	con	con ver	con ver sa	conversation
disagreement	dis	dis a	dis a gree	disagreement

D. Note the italicized parts of the first word in each column. The words in each column begin and end with the same prefix and suffix, which in every case are pronounced exactly the same. Reading down the columns, pronounce these words as quickly as you can. This practice will help you recognize and sound out words when you meet them in your reading.

*con*duc*tion*	*re*fill*able*	*dis*appoint*ment*
conformation	remarkable	disagreement
condensation	reclaimable	disarmament
conservation	recoverable	disarrangement
concentration	redeemable	displacement

conscription	recallable	disfigurement
contraction	respectable	discouragement
contribution	reliable	disenchantment
conviction	renewable	disengagement
consolidation	restrainable	discontentment

E. The following words contain prefixes and suffixes, but the words are in mixed order. Also, some prefixes and suffixes may be new to you. Practice pronouncing the words as quickly as you can.

dishonorable	resentment	discernment	remorseless
relentless	preoccupation	resistant	readjustment
premeditate	consolidation	distractible	configuration
reconstruction	distributive	preparatory	reelection
protective	recollection	consignment	disqualification
confederation	presumably	prohibitive	constructive
unseasonable	imperfection	automotive	protectorate
implication	discoloration	concealment	unwholesome

F. Each line consists of long words that contain the same prefix and word ending. The prefixes and suffixes are italicized and the words are broken into syllables. Read each line as quickly as you can, blending the syllables into the proper pronunciation of the word.

con ven *tion, con* sti tu *tion, con* ver sa *tion, con* tri bu *tion*

ex am i na *tion, ex* pe di *tion, ex* cep *tion, ex* hi bi *tion*

dis ap point *ment, dis* a gree *ment, dis* arm a *ment, dis* cour age *ment*

re fill a *ble, re* place a *ble,   re* new a *ble, re* pay a *ble*

in ex act *ly, in* sane *ly, in* dis tinct *ly, in* stant *ly*

ABBREVIATIONS

Abbreviations represent a special instance of structural (visual) changes that are found in printed material. Children need to understand the following concepts about abbreviations:

1. They are a short form of writing that represents a longer word or phrase.
2. They are frequently followed by a period.
3. They are not pronounced, but the word the abbreviation stands for is pronounced.

We See	*We Say*	*We See*	*We Say*
Mr.	Mister	Pres.	President
Dr.	Doctor	Gov.	Governor
Ave.	Avenue	St.	Street

One approach for helping children learn and deal with abbreviations is to present a series of related terms, such as measures, language terms, state names, days of the week or names of the month, titles, and so on.

Columns A and B illustrate series; column C presents mixed terms.

A		B		C	
Sunday	Sun.	inch	in.	abbreviated	abbr.
Monday	Mon.	pound	lb.	abbreviation	abbrev.
Tuesday	Tues.	mile	mi.	building	bldg.
Wednesday	Wed.	quart	qt.	plural	pl.
Thursday	Thurs.	square foot	sq. ft.	Northwest	N.W.
Friday	Fri.	yard	yd.	mountain	mt.
Saturday	Sat.	pint	pt.	Boulevard	Blvd.

Directions: Write a number of abbreviations on the chalkboard. Have volunteers give the words the abbreviations represent.

Examples:

Pres.   __President__

Dr.   __Doctor__

Ave.   _____

sq. yd.   _____

Gov.   _____

etc.   _____

St.   _____

U.S.   _____

Directions: Have the children write the abbreviations for the words listed. If they need help, they can choose from the abbreviations in the clue box.

Clue Box				
D.C.	Gov.	Atty.	Prof.	Wk.
Dr.	Bldg.	Ave.	Chap.	Mr.

Mister _____   Doctor _____

Building _____   Governor _____

Professor _____   Week _____

District of Columbia _____   Avenue _____

Chapter _____   Attorney _____

Teacher: "In the blank space under each underlined word, write the abbreviation of that word."

1. Last <u>Monday</u> the <u>President</u> spoke to the <u>Governor</u>.

_____   _____   _____

2. To write the <u>plural</u> of <u>pound</u> add an *s*.

_____   _____

3. The <u>doctor</u> has an office on Elm <u>Avenue</u>.

_____   _____

4. The words <u>mile</u>, <u>foot</u>, and <u>quart</u> are measures.

_____   _____   _____

5. The <u>professor</u> lives on <u>Mountain</u> <u>Boulevard</u>.

_____   _____   _____

RECOGNIZING CONTRACTIONS

In oral language, children both use and understand contractions. In reading, they need to learn the visual patterns involved, along with the following facts about contractions:

- A contraction is a single word that results from combining two or more words.
- A contraction omits one or more letters found in the combining words.
- A contraction contains an apostrophe where a letter or letters have been omitted.
- A contraction carries the same meaning as the long form it represents, but it has its own pronunciation.

Children need practice in seeing and saying the contracted forms so they can eventually master them as sight words. There are three steps in dealing with contractions: (a) seeing words and contractions together, (b) matching words and contractions, and (c) writing contractions.

1. Seeing Words and Contractions Together

Teacher: "Look at the two words in each line of the first column and see how they form a contraction when combined in the second column."

Words	Contractions		Words	Contractions
I am	I'm		do not	don't
you are	you're		does not	doesn't
it is	it's		was not	wasn't
I have	I've		would not	wouldn't
you have	you've		could not	couldn't
they have	they've		should not	shouldn't

2. Matching Words and Contractions

Teacher: "Draw a line from the two words in each row of column A to their contraction in column B."

A	B		A	B
does not	I've		let us	wouldn't
I have	doesn't		would not	let's

do not	can't	was not	I'd
I am	don't	could not	wasn't
cannot	I'm	I would	couldn't

3. Writing Contractions

Teacher: "Write the contraction for each of the following word pairs."

they are	_____	I have	_____
she is	_____	should not	_____
must not	_____	here is	_____
will not	_____	they have	_____

Teacher: "On the blank space following each sentence, write the contraction for the italicized words."

Example:

Bill *cannot* go swimming. <u>can't</u>

1. *We will* be careful with our campfire. _____

2. Sue *did not* brush her teeth after breakfast. _____

3. *Let us* have a sack race. _____

4. They *could not* catch a fish. _____

5. *I have* eaten my lunch already. _____

6. Larry *does not* play in the street. _____

7. *I am* very happy to see you. _____

8. Karen and Jeff *were not* ready to sing. _____

9. This *is not* my house. _____

10. They *do not* seem very friendly. _____

FINDING LITTLE WORDS IN BIG WORDS

In the past, considerable confusion has arisen over a particular practice. It was once quite common, in materials prepared for teachers, to suggest that children be taught to look for little words in big words. The theory was that after children had learned to recognize smaller words, it would be useful to them as readers if they would see these smaller units when they were part of larger words. This, it was alleged, would help children solve or pronounce the larger words.

This practice, of course, has only limited utility or justification. It is justifiable when dealing with compound words or known root words to which prefixes or suffixes have been added. In general, however, the habit of seeing little words in big words will actually interfere with sounding out words in a great many cases; this is true even in beginning reading.

To illustrate, let us look at some of the more common "little words." In each of the following, if children see and pronounce the little word, they cannot arrive at the pronunciation of the word under attack.

at:	bo at	b at h	pl at e	o at	at e	at omic
	r at e	pot at o	co at	at hlete	he at	
as:	bo as t	ple as e	As ia	co as t	as hore	
on:	on e	t on e	d on e	h on ey	st on e	
he:	he at	he lp	c he st	bat he	t he y	w he at
me:	me at	a me n	ca me	sa me	a me nd	

Hundreds of other examples could be added, using the previous list of little words and many others, such as *in, an, it, am, if, us, is, to, up, go, no, lid, are,* and *or.* Little words (or their spellings) occur frequently in larger polysyllabic words, but the pronounceable autonomy of the little words in big words is often lost. Therefore, teaching children to look for little words in big words has little justification from the standpoint of phonic or structural analysis.

ACCENT

Every syllable in polysyllabic words is not spoken with the same force or stress. These variations in stress are called *accent.* The syllable that receives the most stress is said to have the primary accent (*car'* pen ter). Other syllables in a word may have a secondary accent, or syllables may be unaccented (in' vi ta' tion).

Teaching accent is usually reserved for the later stages of word analysis. The majority of words met in beginning reading consist of one or two syllables; longer words are those a child has probably heard or spoken hundreds of times (*yesterday, grandmother, afternoon, tomorrow, telephone*).

Accent is important in using a dictionary when the objective is to determine a word's pronunciation. It is important in reading when children meet words they do not know on sight but have heard and whose meanings they know. For instance, if children have heard or used the words *celebration* and *appendicitis* but do not recognize the printed symbols, they may distort the pronunciation through improper syllabication: *cē leb' ra tion* rather than *cĕl e' bra tion;* or improper accent: *ap' pen di ci tis.*

Skills to be taught include the following:

1. How to read primary and secondary accent marks in the dictionary
2. The habit of trying different soundings if the first attempt does not result in a known word
3. The use of clues or rules of accent in attempting the pronunciation of words

These are some of the clues and rules:

In compound words, the primary accent usually falls on (or within) the first word (sail' boat, wolf' hound, fish' er man, door' way).

In two-syllable words containing a double consonant, the accent usually falls on the first syllable (cop' per, mil' lion, pret' ty, val' ley, sud' den).

When *ck* ends a syllable, that syllable is usually accented (chick' en, rock' et, pack' age, nick' el, mack' er el).

Syllables comprised of a consonant plus *le* are usually not accented (*ble, cle, dle, gle, ple, tle*).

Many of the instances covered by the preceding rules might be summarized under one inclusive generalization: In two-syllable root words, the accent usually falls on the first syllable—except when the second syllable contains two vowels (pa rade', sur prise', sus tain', ma chine', sup pose').

Prefixes and suffixes are usually not accented (lone' ly, un hap' pi ly, re fresh' ment, dis re spect' ful, re tract' a ble).

Two-syllable words ending with *y* are usually accented on the first syllable (cit' y, ear' ly, ba' by, can' dy, sto' ry, par' ty, fun' ny, mer' ry, tru' ly).

Shift in Accent

Adding suffixes to some longer words may cause a shift in the primary accent. The words in the left-hand column have the primary accent on the first or second syllables, but in the right-hand column, the accent has shifted.

u' ni verse	u ni ver' sal
mi' cro scope	mi cro scop' ic
vac' ci nate	vac ci na' tion
ac' ci dent	ac ci den' tal
con firm'	con fir ma' tion

We can thus generalize that in many longer words, the primary accent falls on the syllable before the suffix. Exception: In most cases, the primary accent falls two syllables before the suffix *-ate:* ag' gra vate, dom' i nate, ed' u cate, hes' i tate, med' i tate, and op' er ate.

Homographs and accent shift. Homographs are words with identical spellings, different meanings, and, in some cases, different pronunciations. Note in the following sentences that usage or context determines the pronunciation. Changes may occur in accent or in both accent and syllabication. For example, present = pre/sent' or pres'/ent; content = con/tent' or con'/tent:

1. The mayor was *present* to *present* the awards.
2. The editor was not *content* with the *content* of the article.
3. Always be careful to *address* the letter to the correct *address*.

The following words can be used in exercises when context is provided:

protest—protest	annex—annex
perfect—perfect	rebel—rebel
convict—convict	object—object
permit—permit	contract—contract
excuse—excuse	produce—produce
subject—subject	conduct—conduct

STRESS ON WORDS WITHIN SENTENCES

When working on the accents of syllables within words, one might point out the parallel of stress on words within sentences. While this is not usually seen as a word-analysis skill, it is a most important factor in mastering the reading process. Concomitant teaching of accent and stress may help children understand both concepts. Simple sentences might be placed on the board. Children should read the sentences, place added stress on each underlined word, and note the effect of the stress on the melody of the sentence:

This is very bad news.
This is very bad _news_.
This is _very_ bad news.
This is very _bad_ news.

USE OF THE DICTIONARY AS A WORD ATTACK SKILL

As children become independent readers, they are likely to meet a number of words that

They do not know or use in their speaking vocabularies

They cannot easily solve by applying phonic generalizations

Because the dictionary is a source for pronunciation of words, certain dictionary skills are, in effect, word analysis skills. Effective use of the dictionary involves learning the speech equivalents of visual symbols, including primary and secondary accent marks and other diacritical marks, such as the macron (-) (make = māk), the breve (˘) (ăt), and the schwa (ə) (ten dər).

Different dictionaries and glossaries in textbooks may use a variety of symbols, or phonetic spellings, all of which will have to be mastered. For example,

technique: tek nēk, tĕk nēk, tek neek
temperament: tem' pər ə mənt, tĕm pēr ment

(For a discussion of the schwa sound, see Chapter 6).

Children should be taught word attack skills using the same pronunciation key that is found in the dictionaries they use. The dictionary will be of little value in arriving at the correct pronunciation of words if these various symbols are not mastered.

SUMMARY

Teaching the decoding process involves more than just letter-sound relationships. Children must also learn to recognize and respond quickly to a number of frequently occurring visual patterns found in English writing. These include inflectional endings, plurals, contractions, abbreviations, prefixes, and suffixes.

After many experiences with affixes (which are also syllables), successful readers develop the ability to treat these word parts as units rather than decoding the same set of letters separately each time they encounter the letters. Thus, in teaching structural analysis skills, the goal is to provide experiences that lead children to this type of behavior. The structural changes that occur over and over in English writing must be instantly recognized. Fortunately, many of these high-frequency affixes have a high degree of consistency in both their visual patterns and sounds.

REFERENCES

Adams, M. J. (1990). *Beginning to read: Thinking and learning about print.* Cambridge, MA: MIT Press.

Bailey, M. H. (1967). The utility of phonic generalizations in grades one through six. *Reading Teacher, 20,* 413–418.

Bloomfield, L., & Barnhart, C. (1961). *Let's read: A linguistic approach.* Detroit, MI: Wayne State University Press.

Bruner, J. S. (1972). Address to the International Reading Association Convention. Detroit.

Burmeister, L. E. (1968). Vowel pairs. *Reading Teacher, 21,* 445–452.

Burrows, A., & Lourie, Z. (1963) When two vowels go walking. *Reading Teacher, 17,* 79–82.

Chall, J. S. (1989). Learning to read: The great debate 20 years later. *Phi Delta Kappan, 70,* 521–538.

Clymer, T. (1963). The utility of phonic generalizations in the primary grades. *Reading Teacher, 16,* 252–258.

Cunningham, P. M. (1990). The names test: A quick assessment of decoding ability. *Reading Teacher, 44,* 124–129.

Cunningham, P. M., and Cunningham, J. W. (1992). Making words: Enhancing the inverted spelling-decoding connection. *Reading Teacher, 46,* 106–115.

Downing, J. A. (1963). *Experiments with Pitman's initial teaching alphabet in British schools.* New York: Initial Teaching Alphabet Publications.

Downing, J. A. (May, 1965). Common misconceptions about i.t.a. *Elementary English, 42,* 492–501.

Downing, J. A. (December, 1967). Can i.t.a. be improved? *Elementary English, 44,* 849–855.

Early, M. (1993). What ever happened to . . .? *Reading Teacher, 46,* 302–308.

Emans, R. (1967). The usefulness of phonic generalizations above the primary grades. *Reading Teacher, 20,* 419–425.

Flesch, R. (1955). *Why Johnny can't read.* New York: Harper.

Fries, C. C. (1963). *Linguistics and reading.* New York: Holt, Rinehart, & Winston.

Gattengo, C. (1962). *Words in color.* Chicago: Learning Materials.

Goodman, K. S. (1992). I didn't found whole language. *Reading Teacher, 46,* 188–198.

Heilman, A. W. (1977). *Principles and practices of teaching reading,* 4th ed. Columbus, OH: Merrill.

Manning, J. C. (1995). Ariston metron. *Reading Teacher, 48,* 650–659.

Moustafa, M. (1993). Recoding in whole language reading instruction. *Language Arts, 70,* 483–487.

Newman, J. M., & Chruch, S. M. (1990). Myths of whole language. *Reading Teacher, 44,* 20–26.

Oaks, R. E. (1952). A study of the vowel situations in a primary vocabulary. *Education, 72,* 604–617.

Pollard, R. (1889). *Pollard's synthetic method.* Chicago: Western Publishing House.

Programmed reading (n.d.). Webster Division, McGraw-Hill.

Reading Teacher. (1991). Beginning to read: A critique by literacy professionals and a response by Marilyn Jager Adams, *44,* 366–395.

Richgels, D. J., Poremba, K. J., & McGee, L. M. (1996). Kindergartners talk about print: Phonemic awareness in meaningful contexts. *Reading Teacher, 49,* 632–642.

Samuels, S. J. (1988). Decoding and automaticity: Helping poor readers become automatic at word recognition. *Reading Teacher, 41,* 756–760.

Smith, F. (1973). *Psycholinguistics and reading.* New York: Holt, Rinehart, & Winston.

Smith, N. B. (1934). *American reading instruction.* New York: Silver Burdett.

Spiegel, D. L. (1992). Blending whole language and systematic direct instruction. *Reading Teacher, 46,* 38–44.

Stahl, S. A. (1992). Saying the "P" word: Nine guidelines for exemplary phonics instruction. *Reading Teacher, 45,* 618–625.

Stahl, S. A., Osborn, J., & Lehr, F. (1990). *Beginning to read: Thinking and learning about print—a summary.* Champaign, IL: University of Illinois.

Stanovich, K. E. (1993). Romance and reality. *Reading Teacher, 47,* 280–291.

Strickland, D. S. (1994). Reinventing our literacy programs: Books, basics, balance. *Reading Teacher, 48,* 294–302.

Veatch, J. (1996). From the vantage of retirement. *Reading Teacher, 49,* 510–516.

Walmsley, S. A., and Adams, E. L. (1993). Realities of whole language. *Language Arts, 70,* 272–280.

Yopp, H. K. (1992). Developing phonemic awareness in young children. *Reading Teacher, 45,* 696–703.

Yopp, H. K. (1995). A test for assessing phonemic awareness in young children. *Reading Teacher, 49,* 20–28.

INDEX